Quiet Evolution

QUIET EVOLUTION

A Study of the
Educational System of Ontario

ROBIN S. HARRIS

UNIVERSITY OF TORONTO PRESS

© University of Toronto Press 1967
Reprinted 2017
ISBN 978-0-8020-6067-9 (paper)

DR. Z. S. PHIMISTER, Deputy Minister of Education for the Province of Ontario, died on November 20, 1966 while this book was in press. He found the time in June to read the essay on which the book is based, and we talked for several hours about it in the quiet of his home. His comments—and this was typical of him—were concerned not with the details but with the over-all interpretation of the Ontario educational system and with the proposals for its improvement. I made no notes of this conversation, but I am sure that what he said was taken into account when I wrote the final draft.

As it happened this was the last of many kindnesses done to me by Dr. Phimister in the eight years I knew him. I owe him a great deal and not least my interest in and concern about Ontario's educational system. To the improvement of this system Dr. Phimister devoted his working life.

With Mrs. Phimister's permission, I dedicate this book to his memory.

Introduction

La Révolution tranquille is the phrase generally used to refer to the social and economic changes which have been taking place in the province of Quebec since about 1960. Some will argue that the adjective is inaccurate, that "quiet," and even less "tranquil," is not precisely the word to use when referring to either the current mood of the province or the actual events which constitute the landmarks of the Revolution itself. But few will quarrel with the choice of the noun. Many of the changes are of a sufficiently fundamental nature—involving, for example, a new relationship of church and state—to constitute a new order; the movement, therefore, calls for a descriptive term which implies an abrupt change of direction or an essentially new orientation. In constitutional terms it is a matter of introducing new legislative acts, not of amending old ones.

Nowhere in the context of Quebec's recent history is the word "revolutionary" more apt than in reference to the changes that are being made in the province's educational system. Here, unquestionably, the changes are fundamental and profound. The whole system is in the process of being restructured as the state takes over effective control. If proof is required, one need only note that for at least a century and a half the classical college has been the keystone of the

Quebec system and that under the new dispensation the classical college in effect disappears.

The new system has been drafted by the Royal Commission of Inquiry on Education in Quebec which was appointed in 1961 with Monseigneur Alphonse-Marie Parent, Vice-Rector of l'Université Laval, as Chairman. The system is described and its introduction justified in the five volumes of the Commission's report which have been published in the course of the past two years. This is, of course, simply a report: none of its over six hundred recommendations has any practical significance unless adopted as policy by the Quebec government. However, enough of the major recommendations of the report have been not only accepted in principle but implemented by legislative action to ensure that the system proposed by the Parent Commission will be the one which has been adopted in the province of Quebec by 1970.

The educational situation in Ontario is both similar and different. Changes as radical as many of those which are taking place in Quebec have been introduced in Ontario during the past several years: a reorganization of the Department of Education, the creation of a Department of University Affairs, the abolition of the school section, the establishment of new post-secondary institutions called colleges of applied arts and technology, and the reform of Grade 13. Others are in prospect: the abolition of the Grade 13 departmental examinations, the requirement that all elementary school teachers must have a university degree, and the establishment of an educational television network. But, though there is great interest in such changes, their full significance is not appreciated, and each is regarded as being either more radical or less radical than in fact it is. This is because each innovation tends to be viewed in isolation. There has been no Parent Commission in Ontario to provide a master plan by which the series of specific measures undertaken during the past two or three years can be interpreted. But the fact that there is no convenient blueprint to consult when estimating the significance of Innovation A or Adjustment B does not reduce their significance. It does mean that a greater effort has to be made to view them in perspective.

Unlike the Quebec system, the Ontario educational system is not being restructured in any fundamental way. The changes are evolutionary rather than revolutionary; they are developments that are consistent with the rationale of the system as it has evolved in the course of one hundred and fifty years. They represent less a break with tradition than a logical expansion of it. To return to the constitutional metaphor, they do take the form of amendments to existing acts rather than, as in Quebec, of the substitution of new acts for old.

The key to understanding the nature and the significance of the changes that are being made in the educational system of Ontario is an appreciation of the dimensions and the organization of the system itself. The main purpose of this study is to supply that key. I propose to describe the system as it exists today, to identify those features of it which are either unique or distinctive, and to explain by reference to their historical development how these unusual features have come to occupy the position in the system which they do. This, as I say, is my main purpose, essentially the presentation of a considerable number of facts. But I also intend to make some comments on the facts thus presented. There are disadvantages to the present approach to education in Ontario as well as advantages, and it is important that these be clearly recognized. The educational system of Ontario is one of the province's greatest strengths, but it has become such a vast complex that it is exposed to the danger of fragmentation and compartmentalization. The basic problem is one of co-ordination, of making sure not only that the left hand knows what the right hand is doing, but that they pull—or push—in the same direction. There is a good deal of evidence that the parts of the system are at times working if not at cross purposes to at least in ignorance of each other, and this disturbs me. I shall conclude, therefore, with some criticisms of the system as it now operates and with some suggestions as to how it ought to evolve in the future. In particular I shall argue the need for closer liaison between government departments and I shall propose the establishment of regional educational councils throughout the province as a means of breaking down the barriers which, by isolating teachers in one type of institution from their colleagues in all others, inhibit a concentrated attack on the problems of education as a whole.

The study is based on an essay on the educational system of Ontario which, in April 1965, I was asked to prepare for the Royal Commission on Bilingualism and Biculturalism. Substantial portions of the essay, which I submitted to the Commission in January 1966, have been incorporated in the present work. The material has, however, been rearranged, the statistics of the academic year 1965–6 have been substituted for those of 1964–5, and both the introductory and concluding chapters have been rewritten. I am grateful to the Royal Commission for permission to adapt the material to this new form. Needless to say the views expressed are my own, and not those of the Commission.

I want to acknowledge the assistance I have received from representatives of the various government departments which, as will become apparent, are directly involved in the Ontario educational system; they have supplied me with statistics and answered my questions quickly and with good humour. I am grateful also to the following persons who, having read all or part of either the original essay or the final manuscript, have made corrections, or suggested improvements: Dr. Willard Brehaut, Ontario Institute for

Studies in Education; Dr. Corbin Brown, formerly Registrar, Department of Education; Miss Beverley Carter, Innis College, University of Toronto; Edward M. Davidson, Director of Admissions, University of Toronto; Mrs. Frances Ireland, Research Assistant, Office of the President, University of Toronto; Mrs. David G. Kilgour; William J. McCordic, Executive Secretary, Metropolitan School Board of Toronto; Professor H. Blair Neatby, Supervisor, Educational Research Programme, Royal Commission on Bilingualism and Biculturalism; Professor G. B. Payzant, Department of Philosophy, University of Toronto; and E. E. Stewart, Assistant Deputy Minister, Department of University Affairs.

RSH

September 1966

Contents

TABLES

CHARTS

Quiet Evolution

The Educational System of Ontario in 1965-1966

The first thing to recognize when discussing the educational system of Ontario is that it is not synonymous with the activities of the Department of Education nor even with the combination of the activities of that department and those of the recently established Department of University Affairs. It is true that between them these two departments have direct, or indirect, jurisdiction over more than 95 per cent of the educational work carried on in the province but it is also true that at least seven other government departments are also parts of the system. Three departments—Agriculture, the Attorney-General, and Lands and Forests—operate schools of their own. The Department of Health is indirectly responsible for sixty-two hospital schools of nursing, forty-five training centres for nursing assistants, and also, in association with the Department of Education, for teaching the mentally retarded. The Department of Labour supervises all apprenticeship programmes. The approximately twelve hundred boys and girls in the twelve Ontario Training Schools directed by the Department of Reform Institutions are, in effect, full-time students. The Department of the Provincial Secretary is concerned with the integration of new Canadians into the province's economic, social, and cultural life. I say *at least* seven other departments, besides Education and University Affairs, form part of the system; there may be more. Welfare, for example, in conjunction with the federal government has some responsibility for the welfare—and hence the education—of treaty Indians. It could also be argued that, since all government departments like all large businesses have training programmes of a more or less formal nature for their employees, each department is automatically in the educational business. But this is to stretch the term, "educational system," to absurd lengths. In outlining the dimensions of the Ontario system I shall ignore all such in-service training programmes even when, as is the case with the Ontario Provincial Police College, established by the Attorney-General's Department at Aylmer in 1949, they have adopted an institutionalized form.

The fact that the system involves so many government departments is one indication of both its importance and its range. Another is the number of people in the province who are directly concerned with its day-to-day operation—about one person in every three. The population of Ontario in 1965 was just under 7,000,000 of whom over 1,750,000 were full-time students, at least 75,000 were full-time teachers, and perhaps 20,000 were occupied as non-teaching employees of educational institutions (3,000 by the Toronto Board of Education alone). The educational system also involved directly over 20,000 persons who were serving as school trustees, as members of home and school association executives, or as governors of private schools or universities. It was also of indirect but intimate concern to many of the parents of the 1,750,000 students and many of the husbands or wives of the 75,000 teachers. Finally, it should be noted that every Ontario taxpayer is a supporter of its educational system.

I propose now to outline the system by describing the educational work carried on by each of the government departments concerned. I shall begin with the Department of Education, move on to the Department of University Affairs, and conclude with the others.

THE DEPARTMENT OF EDUCATION

Central Authority

The person most responsible for the educational system of Ontario is the elected member of the Legislature who is assigned the portfolio of Education by the Premier. As Minister of Education, he is directly responsible for all the activities of the Department of Education; these embrace all elementary and secondary education, all teacher training, all vocational training that is not the specific responsibility of another government department, the public libraries of the province, and a major share of adult education. Up to the end of 1964 the affairs of the department were conducted under his supervision by a chief director, two deputy ministers, a registrar, and eight superintendents, each responsible for a particular branch: Elementary Education, Secondary Education, Teacher Education, Technological and Trades Training, Special Services (audio visual aids, school railway cars, guidance, etc.), Curriculum, Professional Development (in-service training of teachers), and Business Administration. By a major reorganization which became effective in 1965, a single deputy minister assumed general responsibility for the whole department, divided into three areas, for each of which an assistant deputy minister became directly responsible. These three areas are:

(1) *Instruction*, embracing the work of both elementary and secondary schools (under the previous organization these branches had been separate);

(2) *Provincial Schools and Further Education,* including the teachers' colleges, the institutes of technology, and the vocational centres (which are to be absorbed in the new colleges of applied arts and technology), the schools for the deaf and blind, and adult education generally; and

(3) *Administration.*

The minister has an executive assistant and there is an Educational Policy and Development Council which, unencumbered by any direct responsibility for administering anything, is free to explore ways in which the department's work can be improved in efficiency and expanded in scope. Chart 1 outlines the present organization of the Department.

Chart 1 also calls attention to what are called Ministerial Agencies; these are bodies established by legislative act which, though in most respects independent of the Department of Education, come under the minister's supervision. The Teachers' Superannuation Commission administers teachers' pensions. The Ryerson Polytechnical Institute, which until 1964 was the direct responsibility of the department, now has its own Board of Governors. The Ontario Colleges of Education at Toronto and London, which provide for the training of secondary school teachers, are entirely financed by the Department of Education but, being, in effect, faculties of the Universities of Toronto and Western Ontario respectively, come under the jurisdiction of the Board of Governors and the Senate of these institutions. The Defence Training Board supervises services provided for the federal government—the board hires and pays the salaries (from funds provided by the Department of National Defence) of instructors in army and air force schools located in Ontario. The Ontario Council for the Arts is a body of twelve persons appointed by the Government "to promote the study and enjoyment of and the production of works in the Arts"; it has sole responsibility for the disbursement of funds voted by the Legislature for this purpose. During the first two years of its existence (1963–4, 1964–5) the annual grant was $300,000 and amounts ranging from $250 to $50,000 were made to fifty-eight organizations. The 1965–6 grant was $500,000.

Elementary and Secondary Schools

Education is compulsory in Ontario from the age of six to sixteen. A child normally enters Grade 1 in September of the calendar year in which he becomes six and he normally is required to attend school until June of the calendar year in which he becomes sixteen; any student who has completed Grade 12 before this age can be excused from attendance and the same privilege can, under certain conditions, be granted to children who are at least fourteen. No child is required to attend kindergarten. It is up to each local school board to decide whether or not this service is provided; if it is there is no tuition fee and the children are admitted normally at age five, but in some cases at age four. Schools are officially described either as elementary schools or as secondary schools— these are the only classifications used in the Minister's *Annual Report*. There are eight grades in the elementary school and five in the secondary. But the elementary school also includes the kindergarten year if it is offered and some elementary schools are permitted to offer the work of Grades 9 and 10. Furthermore, in some municipalities there are three types of school rather than two: junior public schools (kindergarten and Grades 1 to 6); either senior public schools (7 and 8) or junior high schools (7 to 9 or 7 to 10); and either secondary schools (9 to 13) or senior high schools (10 to 13 or 11 to 13). Thus, in addition to the normal 8:5 division, one also finds 6:2:5, 6:3:4, and 6:4:3.

CHART 1 Organization, Department of Education, 1965

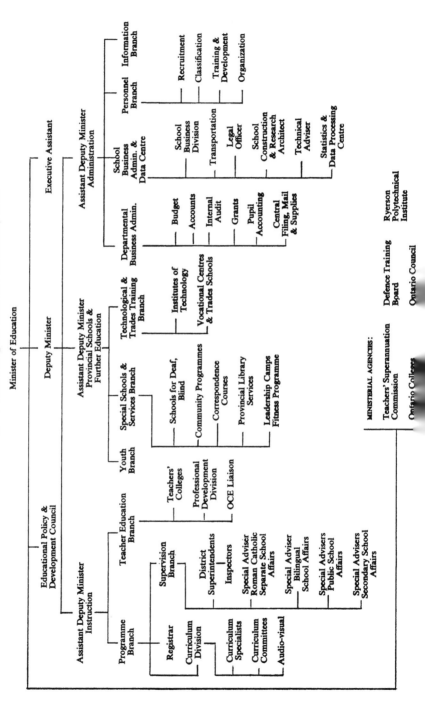

There are two types of publicly supported elementary schools, the public or non-sectarian and the separate (normally Roman Catholic).[1] Every ratepayer in the province is a public school supporter unless he declares himself to be a separate school supporter in which case his share of the property taxes collected for the support of the elementary schools goes to the local separate school board and his children attend the separate schools. There are no publicly supported separate secondary schools; the children of both public and separate school supporters have the right to attend the public secondary schools. A parent is at liberty to send a child of compulsory school age to a private school, which charges tuition fees, rather than to a public or separate school which does not, but if he does so he is still required to pay his school taxes. Private schools are required to register with the Department of Education, but departmental supervision is limited to Grades 11 and 12 where inspection is required in order that the private school can recommend students for the Department of Education Secondary School Graduation Diploma. Private school students are, of course, at liberty to write the matriculation examinations, administered by the Department of Education, which are the basis for admission to universities and teachers' colleges. The Department of Education itself conducts two residential schools for the deaf (at Belleville and Milton) and one for the blind (at Brantford); the course of study offered in these schools is that of the equivalent grade of the elementary or secondary school.

For residents of the province who, for health, geographic, or occupational reasons, are unable to attend a regular school, the department offers the elementary and secondary programmes through correspondence courses provided without charge. In 1965–6 over 25,000 persons were enrolled with the Correspondence Division.

There is a single course of study for the eight grades of

the elementary school which outlines the subjects to be taken in each grade and the approximate proportion of time to be allotted to each. But special provisions are made for French-speaking pupils in what are known as "bilingual schools." In 1965, 425 of the public and separate schools of Ontario were officially so recognized by the Minister of Education and together they enrolled 79,790 pupils, of whom 4,584 were in Grades 9 and 10. The normal procedure in bilingual schools is to conduct kindergarten and the first two grades entirely in French, to introduce English halfway through Grade 3, and to devote an equal amount of time to each language from Grade 5 through to 8. In the English-speaking elementary schools, French is not a required subject, but it can be introduced for a maximum of one hundred minutes per week if the minister's approval is obtained and a teacher who is genuinely fluent in French is available. In 1965, 13.6 per cent of the English-speaking elementary school pupils in the province were receiving instruction in oral French—the comparable figure in 1962 was 6.7, 9.3 in 1963, and in 1964 11.7. Some school boards introduce French at the Grade 3 level, others at 4, 5, 6, or 7. The Minister has announced that French is to be made a compulsory subject in Grades 7 and 8.

In the secondary school there are four distinct programmes:

(1) A one- or two-year programme for students who, at the age of fifteen, have not reached the standard expected for the completion of Grade 8;

(2) A two-year programme for students who have completed Grade 8, who are fourteen years old and who intend, with their parents' consent, to leave school and enter employment in two year's time;

(3) A four-year programme ending at Grade 12; and

(4) A five-year programme ending at Grade 13.

The four- and five-year programmes are offered in each

of three branches: arts and science; business and commerce; science, technology, and trades.

The language of instruction in the secondary schools is English, but school boards can obtain permission to use French as the language of instruction in Latin, history, geography, and in the special course, *Français*, which is an alternative to "French" taken by English-speaking pupils. *Français* has been an official course since 1927; teaching the other subjects in French is a relatively new policy and it is one which is dependent for its implementation upon the availability of textbooks in French which correspond to those provided in English for the regular course. The teaching of Latin in French has been permitted since 1962, of history and geography since 1965.

The Secondary School Graduation Diploma is awarded on successful completion of any Grade 12 programme, the Secondary School Honour Graduation Diploma on completion of a Grade 13 programme. Secondary schools which offer only the arts and science branches are called "academic schools," while those offering only business and commerce and/or science, technology, and trades are called "vocational schools." A school offering arts and science and either or both of the others is called a "composite school." Included among the academic schools are a small number of the continuation schools which were established at the turn of the century to make secondary education available in small communities. The number of these schools, which normally have a staff of two to four teachers, is steadily declining; the development of district high schools to which the students commute by bus has rendered them obsolete.

The publicly supported schools of the province are owned and operated by local school boards of which there are four types: *public school boards* and *separate school boards*, which are concerned respectively with public and separate schools; *high school boards* which are concerned with public

secondary schools; and *boards of education* which are concerned with both public elementary and public secondary
schools. Except for the high school boards, to which trustees
are appointed by municipal councils and by public and
separate school boards, the members of school boards are
elected by the local ratepayers. A board of education can
be established only where the areas of jurisdiction of elementary and secondary school boards coincide. A separate
school board has the right to appoint one or two members
to the board of education which owns and operates the
public secondary schools which the children of separate
school supporters attend.

Responsibility for the schools is shared by the local school
board and the Department of Education. The school board
is responsible for building and maintaining the schools
required for the population within its jurisdiction, for providing the necessary supplies, and for engaging and paying
the teachers. The Department of Education is responsible
for the training and certifying of the teachers, for the
authorization of textbooks, and for defining the course of
study.

There was a time when defining the course of study involved the prescription of almost every detail, but today
detailed directives are limited to the subjects studied in
Grade 13 where the requirements of the university matriculation examinations render this necessary. In the case
of kindergarten, which it will be recalled school boards
are not required to provide, the department contents itself
with recommending a programme for the guidance of
teachers and boards. For Grades 1 to 12 there is an outline
of the course or courses of study, but it is intentionally a
general outline and there is considerable opportunity for
variety in the treatment of a given subject from school to
school. These general outlines, which are the responsibility
of the Department of Education Curriculum Division, are

in fact the product of committees upon which classroom teachers and principals are well represented.

The schools are financed by a combination of local taxes and legislative grants. The legislative grant to an individual school is administered by the Department of Education according to a series of formulae which are issued annually before the local tax rate is established. The local school board determines the amount of money it requires for capital expenditure and maintenance and, having taken into account the amount available to it from the legislative grant, it works out the amount to be raised from the local property tax. This amount it reports to the municipal council which is required to raise by taxation the amount needed for maintenance. Except in rural school sections where the approval of the ratepayers for any capital expenditure is mandatory, the municipal council can either approve the school board's capital figure or submit it to the ratepayers for approval. Thus, the maintenance of existing schools is everywhere enforced by law, but the construction of new schools may be subject to specific endorsement by the local citizens.

The Department of Education's influence over events at the local level is partly determined by its control of the legislative grants and partly by the related power of inspection. Grants can be withheld unless the department's regulations are fulfilled. Moreover, the department is able to encourage local school boards to adopt measures which can be expected to improve the educational programme by offering additional grants which will pay for all or a sizable portion of the increased expenditures. But the school board is normally free *not* to accept the grant and thus *not* to introduce the proposed measure.

A school board's decision to adopt a measure proposed by the department will be determined in large measure by the persuasive powers of the local inspector. In the old days the inspector was an official sent out by the Department of Education to see that the schools were being properly run, but today his role is much more accurately described by the term "supervisor." A great many school boards appoint and pay their own inspectors. Whether appointed locally or assigned to an area by the department, the inspector, being the representative of the minister and the department, has the responsibility of insuring that departmental regulations are carried out. He is, however, essentially the adviser of the teachers and the board and much more concerned with the advancement of education in the area—for example, by the raising of educational standards—than with checking on this and on that.

Until very recently, inspection of elementary schools was carried out under the direction of the Superintendent of Elementary Schools and inspection of secondary schools under the direction of the Superintendent of Secondary Schools. But, in the reorganization of the department which took effect in 1965, a Superintendent of Supervision (who reports to the Assistant Deputy Minister in charge of Instruction) assumed responsibility for the inspection of schools at both levels. The new arrangement is designed to increase the amount of co-ordination between elementary and secondary education. It is also designed to increase the amount of local autonomy or, perhaps we should say, to decrease the emphasis upon centralized authority. The province has now been divided into the following ten areas, and an Area Superintendent of Supervision has been appointed in each:

Northwestern Ontario
    Thunder Bay, Rainy River, and Kenora districts, with headquarters at Port Arthur;
Mid-northern Ontario
    Algoma, Sudbury and Manitoulin districts, with headquarters at Sudbury;

Northeastern Ontario
Cochrane, Muskoka, Nipissing, Parry Sound, and Timis-
kaming districts, with headquarters at North Bay;
Western Ontario
Elgin, Essex, Huron, Kent, Lambton, and Middlesex
counties, with headquarters at London;
Mid-western Ontario
Brant, Bruce, Grey, Norfolk, Oxford, Perth, Waterloo, and
Wellington counties, with headquarters at Waterloo;
Niagara
Haldimand, Lincoln, Welland, and Wentworth counties,
with headquarters at St. Catharines;
West Central Ontario
Dufferin, Halton, Peel, and Simcoe counties; the City of
Toronto and the municipalities of Metropolitan Toronto
situated wholly to the west of Yonge Street, with head-
quarters at Toronto;
East Central Ontario
Durham, Ontario, Victoria, and York counties; the Town-
ship of North York, and the municipalities of Metropolitan
Toronto situated wholly to the east of Yonge Street, with
headquarters at Don Mills;
Eastern Ontario
Frontenac, Haliburton, Hastings, Leeds, Lennox and
Addington, Northumberland, Peterborough, and Prince
Edward counties, with headquarters at Kingston;
Ottawa Valley
Carleton, Dundas, Stormont, Glengarry, Grenville, Lanark,
Prescott, Russell, and Renfrew counties, with headquarters
at Eastview.

The Department of Education was also responsible in
1965–6 for ninety-three special schools for mentally retarded children which together enrolled 3,364 pupils. These
are schools attended by children who live in their own
homes and should not be confused with the four residential
Ontario Hospital Schools which come under the authority
of the Department of Health.[2] The stimulus to establish
these day schools originated with parents, who formed

associations for this purpose, the first being opened at Kirkland Lake in 1947. By 1954 there were nineteen, and at
this point the Department of Education began to provide
grants to assist in their financing. Legislation approved in
January 1965 provides for the establishment of a Retarded
Children's Education Authority in any community where
there are ten eligible children, the authority consisting of
six members, two appointed by the local parents' association
and four by the municipal council. The local association
must provide for 50 per cent of the cost of the school building, the remainder being provided by the Department of
Education. The department pays 80 per cent of their operating costs and the municipal council provides the remaining
20 per cent. Since 1957 the department has been offering a
special five-week course in the summer for teachers of retarded children.

Teacher Training

The Department of Education maintains thirteen teachers'
colleges for the training of elementary school teachers and
two colleges of education for the training of secondary
school teachers. The latter are operated under agreements
between the Minister of Education and one of the universities of the province—the Ontario College of Education
in Toronto with the University of Toronto, Althouse College in London with the University of Western Ontario. A
third college of education, to be called McArthur College,
will open at Kingston in 1967 under an agreement with
Queen's University. Several of the teachers' colleges are
located on, or in close proximity to, university campuses,
but none, not even the University of Ottawa Teachers'
College, come under the control of the university in question. Two of the teachers' colleges—the University of
Ottawa Teachers' College and Sudbury Teachers' College

—are exclusively concerned with preparing teachers for bilingual schools.

There are five types of elementary school teacher certificates; the Second Class Certificate, and the Elementary School Teacher's Certificate Standards 1, 2, 3, and 4. All the teachers' colleges prepare students for the Elementary School Teacher's Certificate Standard 1. For many years students qualified for this certificate either by taking a two-year course from Grade 12 or a one-year course from Grade 13, but in 1964 the two-year course was withdrawn and applicants are now accepted only for the one-year course. On completing his course the student receives an Interim Certificate; this becomes a permanent certificate upon the recommendation of the department inspector after two years of successful teaching. The teacher can proceed from Standard 1 to Standards 2, 3, and 4 by way of summer courses and university study; the equivalent of a first university year is required for Standard 2, of two university years for Standard 3, and a bachelor's degree is required for Standard 4. It is also possible at the Ontario College of Education, Toronto, to qualify for the Standard 4 Certificate, by taking what is known as the elementary school option in the programme offered to candidates for a secondary school certificate.

The Second Class Certificate has been offered at the University of Ottawa Teachers' College for many years and by the Sudbury Teachers' College since its establishment in 1963. The programme has been a one-year course from Grade 12. It was replaced at the University of Ottawa Teachers' College in September 1966 by a two-year course from Grade 12 leading to the Elementary School Teacher's Certificate. The Sudbury Teachers' College will follow suit in September 1967.

For secondary school teachers there are four types of certificate: the High School Assistant's Certificate Type B, for which the admission requirement is an approved university degree; the High School Assistant's Certificate Type A (Specialist), for which the admission requirement is an honours BA or BSc degree with at least second class standing; the Vocational Certificate Type B, for which Grade 12 standing and trades experience are required; and the Vocational Certificate Type A (Specialist), for which the permanent Type B Certificate and nine Grade 13 papers are required. A year of full-time study is the normal way of qualifying for each of these certificates, but it is also possible to obtain them through summer courses. As with the elementary school certificates, the secondary school certificates are interim when first issued and become permanent after two years of successful teaching.

Technological and Trades Training

The Department of Education Applied Arts and Technology Branch was responsible in 1965-6 for the administration of five institutes of technology and six vocational centres. Both the institutes of technology and the vocational centres will be absorbed in the colleges of applied arts and technology which were authorized by legislation in March 1965. The technological institutes offer three-year courses in a variety of technologies to students who have completed Grade 12. The vocational centres offer trade, business, and technical courses at the post-secondary level, and also courses of varying length to persons whose secondary education ended at Grade 10. Three of the vocational centres, all located in Toronto, are also called provincial institutes of trades; at these institutes, as will be described in a later section,[3] the Department of Labour's apprenticeship programme is offered. The Department of Education is no longer responsible for the administration of Ryerson Polytechnical Institute, but it continues to supply the funds required for its maintenance and development. In 1965–6, these institutions (including Ryerson) enrolled 9,848 full-time students and over 13,000 in evening classes.

The Applied Arts and Technology Branch is also responsible for the operation in Ontario of the federal government's retraining programme for the unemployed (Canadian Vocation Training Program 5), which in 1965 was carried on in forty-three centres throughout the province, and enrolled about 10,000 people. It also sponsors courses in small business management and in supervisory training.

A good deal of training for particular vocations—for example, secretary, barber, hairdresser, welder—is provided throughout the province by private trade schools which are required to register with the department. In 1965 these numbered 114 and reported a total enrolment of 52,036.

Adult Education

Adult education is one of the two major responsibilities of the Assistant Deputy Minister in charge of Provincial Schools and Further Education, and it is an area which is assuming larger and larger importance. The work of the Provincial Library Service is primarily for the benefit of adults as is much of the evening work carried on by the institutes of technology and vocational centres. Through its Provincial Library Service, the Department of Education provides financial assistance, encouragement, and professional advice to the approximately five hundred public libraries in the province. The legislative grant for 1965 was in the amount of $3,315,838, approximately 20 per cent of the total public library expenditure of $18,000,000. The Provincial Library Service, whose staff includes five professional librarians, publishes the *Ontario Library Review* and maintains a special library for rural communities and rural schools.

Four other branches of the department are active in the field of adult education: Youth, Leadership Training, Physical-Fitness Program, and Community Programs. Three of these have been organized recently but the Community Programs Branch has been active for two decades. The range of its activities may be judged from a quotation from the 1965 Minister's *Annual Report*:

The Community Programs Division assists communities to provide better opportunities for people to use their leisure enjoyably and constructively through recreation and adult education. The assistance to communities involves grants, advice, guidance, leadership training, conferences, seminars, clinics and surveys. The Division works in co-operation with municipal recreation committees; school boards; national, provincial and local organizations; and other departments in the Federal and Provincial Governments. Communications with the municipalities are maintained through a field staff which has offices in Belleville, Dryden, Fort William, Hamilton, Hanover, London, North Bay, Oakville, Ottawa, Toronto and Sudbury. There are also special advisers, working out of the central office, on such matters as art, crafts, drama, music, puppetry, senior citizens, recreation buildings and areas, rural programs, and women's physical fitness activities. In order to make resource material available for community use, the Division produces a number of publications and operates a loan service in drama, music, instructional films, slides and reference books. . . .

Ontario Regulation 92/60 Programs of Recreation, made under The Department of Education Act, provides provincial grants to municipalities that pass the necessary by-law to appoint a municipal recreation authority and conduct or assist local recreation programs. During the year 1965, some 23 municipalities established recreation committees for the first time. There were 117 recreation directors as well as 155 assistant directors employed by Ontario municipalities on a yearly basis. The sum of $725,895 was paid to 356 municipalities to assist in the development of the recreation program.[4]

During 1965 over 16,000 persons attended one or more of 300 courses provided by the Community Programs Branch for leaders of adult groups, and over 6,000 one or more of 120 courses for leaders of special groups.

The Department of Education has been conducting summer courses for high school students at Bark Lake in the Haliburton District since 1947, and at Lake Couchiching since 1948. The course at the Ontario Camp Leadership Centre on Bark Lake is for camp counsellors, the students being selected by the directors of non-profit camps. At the Ontario Athletic Leadership Camp at Longford Mills there is a series of two-week courses; one boy and one girl from each secondary school in the province are eligible to attend. Over one thousand students attended one or other of these camps in the summer of 1965. Under the recent reorganization of the department, this programme has been combined administratively with a programme introduced in 1961–2 which is designed to promote the physical fitness of adults.

The Physical Fitness Program Branch is heavily supported by federal funds. The Department of Education contribution is 40 per cent of a total budget which can extent to $233,000. Approximately 15 per cent is expended on bursaries for students attending undergraduate courses in physical education and recreation at six Ontario universities, 10 per cent on the support of two courses provided at the University of Guelph (a one-year course for university graduates and a three-year course for students with Grade 12), and the remaining 75 per cent on the support of projects sponsored by local communities (for example, the organization of a club) or by provincial organizations (for example, the Ontario Softball Association).

The Youth Branch is an entirely new venture which was launched on January 1st, 1964, and it is still very much in the exploratory or planning stage. Its general terms of reference are the special problems of young adults in a changing world, and its immediate concern is their identification. The branch is developing a staff of research officers trained in such fields as economics, education, and sociology.

THE DEPARTMENT OF UNIVERSITY AFFAIRS

The universities of Ontario are chartered institutions and are independent of any government department. The authority at each university is, in all academic matters (degrees, examinations, curricula, instruction), its senate and in financial matters its board of governors or regents. In one instance—the University of Toronto—all appointments to the Board of Governors are made by the Government, but, once appointed, the governor's loyalty is to the board itself. There was a time when the Government of Ontario concerned itself with the day-to-day running of the University of Toronto, but this has not been the case since the passage of the University of Toronto Act of 1906. The tradition that a university is not the creature of the Government is long established in the province.

During the past decade the expenses of universities have risen dramatically, largely, though not exclusively, in response to sharp increases in enrolment, and this has had the effect of greatly increasing the amounts of money required by the universities from public funds. It was this fact which forced the Government to take a more direct interest in the work of the universities and which led to the establishment of a Department of University Affairs. There was no need for such a department twenty years ago when only three universities (Toronto, Queen's, Western Ontario) were in receipt of provincial grants, and when the sums involved were relatively small (just over $5,000,000 in 1947), the matter could be attended to by the Minister of Education or the Premier himself. But by 1965–6, when fifteen chartered institutions received over $150 million in provincial grants for either capital or operating purposes, something more was needed and something more had been supplied.

What has been supplied is, first, a Committee on University Affairs and, second, a Department of University Affairs. The committee, originally established in 1961 as the Advisory Committee on University Affairs, is a group of up to twelve persons appointed by the Government to advise it on all matters concerning the establishment, development, operating, expansion, and financing of universities in Ontario. The Department of University Affairs, created in 1964, is headed by a cabinet minister whose staff includes a deputy minister, an assistant deputy minister, and senior officials responsible for branches concerned with architecture, construction, finance, research, and student aid. The respective roles of the committee and the department have still to be clearly defined, but that the relationship is intimate can be seen from the fact that the deputy minister of the department is the secretary of the committee. Each of the universities which receives public grants submits its proposed budgets to the department.

There are fifteen such universities, one of which, the Osgoode Hall Law School, confines its activity to a single professional field—in 1968 it will become the Faculty of Law of York University. The Department of University Affairs also has jurisdiction over one institution which does not have degree-granting powers—the Ontario College of Art. Basic facts about each of these institutions are provided in Table 1.

There are in Ontario fourteen chartered universities or colleges with degree-granting powers which do not receive grants from the province. All but two of these are associated with one of the institutions listed in Table 1 through an affiliation or federation agreement (Victoria, Trinity, St. Michael's, Knox, and Wycliffe with the University of

Toronto; St. Jerome's with the University of Waterloo; Huron with the University of Western Ontario; Huntingdon, Sudbury, and Thorneloe with Laurentian University of Sudbury; Assumption with Windsor, Université St Paul with Ottawa), and in each case degree-granting power is limited either by the charter or the agreement to the field of theology. There are also two chartered institutions which do not receive a provincial grant but do grant degrees in arts and science, the Royal Military College at Kingston and Waterloo Lutheran University at Waterloo. RMC, which had an enrolment in 1965–6 of 513, is entirely financed by the federal government. Waterloo Lutheran, being under denominational control, is ineligible for a provincial grant and does not fall under the jurisdiction of the Department of University Affairs; its enrolment in 1965–6 was 2,173 undergraduates and 34 graduates. Two professional schools in Toronto, the College of Optometry of Ontario and the Canadian Chiropractic College, also are outside the department's jurisdiction.

A few Ontario universities offer what is called a "Preliminary" or "Qualifying Year" to students who enter with Grade 12 standing, but normal entry is by way of senior matriculation obtained at the conclusion of Grade 13 by writing examinations set and marked by the Department of Education in association with the universities. The BA or BSc degree is offered in both general courses (three-year) and honours courses (four-year). Most professional degrees are granted after a four-year course from Grade 13 (engineering, pharmacy, forestry, physical and health education, etc.), but architecture and dentistry take five and medicine at least six (two premedical years or a BA or BSc, followed by a four-year medical course). Admission to the one year MA or MSc course is normally based on possession of a four-year honours degree; the graduate schools of most Ontario universities require a "make-up" year for applicants with the three-year general degree. Possession of the master's degree is the normal requirement for admission to doctoral programmes, which require at least two years of full-time study.

The Ontario College of Art offers four-year diploma courses with admission from Grade 12.

OTHER GOVERNMENT DEPARTMENTS

Department of Agriculture

From 1874 until July 1st, 1964 when the University of Guelph was established, the Department of Agriculture was entirely responsible for the financing of the Ontario Agricultural College and its associated institutions—the Ontario Veterinary College and the Macdonald Institute—and it continued to be indirectly responsible for them until September 1st, 1965 when the teaching staff ceased to be regarded as part of the civil service and the university assumed responsibility for its buildings from the Department of Public Works. For over seventy-five years both degree and diploma courses in agriculture have been offered at the Guelph campus and, while the former are now the entire responsibility of the University of Guelph and hence, in our present context, within the jurisdiction of the Department of University Affairs, the Department of Agriculture retains financial and academic responsibility for the diploma courses. These are two-year programmes identical in all important respects with the courses offered at two other institutions operated by the department—the Kemptville Agricultural School, established at Kemptville in Eastern Ontario in 1917, and the Western Ontario Agricultural School, established at Ridgetown in 1951. The academic admission requirement to all three of these programmes is Grade 10 (age 18 and at least three months of farm experience are also required), but preference is given to

TABLE 1

The Provincially Supported Universities and Colleges of Ontario 1965–66

	Commenced Instruction	Charter	Prov. grant	Full-time enrolment		Provincial grant (thousands)	
				Undergrad.	Grad.	Operating	Capital
Brock	1964	1964	1963	354		595	1,595
Carleton	1942 as Carleton College	1952	1949	2,737	287	2,675	5,450
Guelph	1864 as Ont. Veterinary Col.	1964	1874	1,890	203	2,350	1,600
	1874 as Ont. Agricultural Col.						
Laurentian	1913 as Collège du Sacré Cœur	1959	1961	938		950	1,949
Lakehead	1948 as Lakehead Technical Inst.	1962	1957	421		500	1,230
McMaster	1857 as Can. Literary Inst.	1887	1948	3,221	520	4,490	6,150
Ontario College of Art	1875 as School of Art and Design		1875	928		215	
Osgoode Hall	1889	1957	1957	523	2		
Ottawa	1848 as Collège St. Joseph	1866	1852–68, 1947	4,869	561	1,625	8,445
Queen's	1842 as Queen's College	1841	1842–68, 1913	4,137	532	4,850	4,875
Toronto	1827 as King's College	1827	1901	14,538	2,945	25,075	18,700
Trent	1962	1962	1962	278	4	625	2,295
Waterloo	1957 as Waterloo College	1959	1956	3,917	511	3,950	10,100
	Associate Faculties						
Western Ontario	1881 as the Western University	1878	1912	6,165	843	5,760	7,050
Windsor	1857 as Collège de l'Assomption	1964	1954	2,175	176	2,175	5,800
York	1960 as U. of T. affiliate	1959	1959	1,447	36	2,250	14,000
TOTAL				48,538	6,620	$58,085	$89,239

Sources: DBS, *Survey of Higher Education*. Part I. *Enrolment in Universities and Colleges, 1965–66*; Ontario Department of University Affairs.

students with Grade 12 and the great majority of those admitted in 1965 had Grade 12 standing or better. In that year the enrolment at Guelph was 251, at Kemptville 210, and at Ridgetown 175—a total of 636. The Kemptville figure includes 89 students in home economics, which like agriculture is a two-year course, and 15 in advanced agricultural mechanics, a one-year course for which the two-year agriculture diploma is prerequisite.

The involvement of the Department of Agriculture in the affairs of the institution at Guelph has by no means ceased with the establishment of the university. The department continues to finance most of the research conducted by the university departments and the university's Extension Department continues to be the means whereby many of the department's services to the farmers of the province are carried out. In many respects the change is one of the accounting procedures; the department now buys services where it earlier had provided a budget.

Department of Health

The Department of Health it not technically responsible for the training of registered nurses and nursing assistants but it is intimately concerned with both programmes.

The nursing profession is responsible for its own regulations and discipline. Internal control by the profession, however, is a fairly recent development. Only in 1951 was the Registered Nurses Association of Ontario given responsibility for registration standards and discipline. Inspection of schools remained the responsibility of the Department of Health until 1962 when it was taken over by the College of Nurses of Ontario, established by the Nurses Act, 1961–2. All registered nurses are members of the college.

To qualify as a registered nurse, one must pass examinations set by the college. The student who completes a degree programme in nursing at a university is well prepared to write these examinations, but most nurses obtain their training at one of the sixty-two hospital schools of nursing which are spread about the province. The funds which support these hospital schools (and also the hospitals of which they are a part) are supplied by the Ontario Hospital Services Commission, a Crown corporation which is independent of the Department of Health but for which the Minister of Health answers in the Legislature. The minister, or his representative, is an *ex officio* member of the Council of the College of Nurses which supervises the work of the hospital schools, and he is thus to some extent involved in its decisions.

The normal programme in the hospital school is a three-year course combining lectures and practical experience, for which the admission requirement is Grade 12. There are also in Toronto three diploma schools of nursing— Nightingale School of Nursing, Toronto General Hospital, and Women's College Hospital—which offer a two-year course from Grade 13 and one, Quo Vadis, which offers a two-year course from Grade 12 for mature students. A three-year course from Grade 12 was introduced at Ryerson Polytechnical Institute in 1964, the academic work being given at the institute and the practical experience at two associated hospitals. The total enrolment in all these schools in 1965 was 8,774.

The College of Nurses is also responsible for the training of nursing assistants. There are forty-five training centres for nursing assistants in the province, thirty of which are located in hospitals, nine in secondary schools, and six in buildings operated directly by the Department of Health Nursing Branch. Together these enrolled 1,473 students in 1965. In all cases the academic admission requirement is Grade 10. In the high school centres, the students, who are regularly enrolled as secondary school students, take a nursing option in Grades 11 and 12, which prepares them to write the provincial examinations for nursing assistants. In the centres directed by the Nursing Branch a ten-month programme is provided, three and one-half months of which is spent at a centre and the remainder gaining practical experience at a hospital. In the hospital centres practical experience and formal instruction are combined over a ten-month period.

The Department of Health was also concerned in 1965-6 with the education of approximately nine hundred mentally retarded children who were in residence at four Ontario Hospital Schools at Chatham, Orillia, Palmerston, and Smith Falls, and at the Children's Psychiatric Research Institute at London. At each the Department of Health provides accommodation for an educational programme and the Department of Education provides the teacher, the teaching equipment, and the teaching programme. The same arrangement has been adopted at two new residential units which opened in September 1966; a Children's Unit at the Ontario Hospital, Port Arthur, and a Mental Retardation Centre at Toronto.

Department of Labour

The Industrial Training Branch of the Department of Labour administers the programmes outlined in the Apprenticeship and Tradesmen Qualification Act of 1964. There are one hundred and twenty-five trades specified in the act, a few—for example, motor vehicle repair, barbering, hairdressing—in which one must be certified or a registered apprentice in order to be employed, and a large number, for example, carpentering, in which certification is optional. The apprenticeship arrangements are identical for both groups. The academic admission requirement is Grade 10. The normal period required to complete the programme is four to five years during which the apprentice spends two periods of ten weeks at a vocational centre or provincial institute of trades. The centres and institutes, which it will be recalled are operated by the Department of Education, have four "classes" each year. In June 1966 the total number of apprentices registered was 12,909, and during 1965 3,240 apprentices took a ten-week period of instruction.

Department of Lands and Forests

When the Department of Lands and Forests opened the Ontario Forest Ranger School at Dorset in 1945 the object was to provide training for young men who were already employed by the department or who would enter its employ on completion of the course. At that time the name was entirely appropriate, as the school produced forest rangers. Today its purpose is to train forestry technicians and conservation officers, and its graduates are as likely to find employment in industry as in government service. Its students come from many Canadian provinces and a proportion come from other countries. The proposal to change its name to the Ontario School of Forestry Technicians has much to recommend it.

The basic course provided is a one-year programme leading to a diploma. To be admitted the student must be eighteen years of age and have Grade 11 standing. But there are more applicants than places (the school is residential) and few students actually admitted during the past few years have had less than Grade 12. The course is divided into three terms of eleven weeks each, and practical field experience is required during the inter-term periods. In 1965 the enrolment was 122.

The school also offers a number of more specialized certificate courses—timber management, forest fire control, fish and wildlife—for its graduates or for persons similarly qualified. These vary in length from three weeks to seven. There is also a junior ranger programme, aimed at high school students, which is offered for six weeks in the summer.

Department of the Provincial Secretary and Citizenship

The Provincial Secretary's Department is responsible for providing courses in English, or French, for immigrants to the province. The classes are almost entirely devoted to the teaching of English to "new Canadians" but are also open to, for example, an immigrant from Quebec who speaks nothing but French. Provision is made for instruction in French in French-speaking communities, but the demand for such classes has been slight.

A class can be organized wherever there are six persons prepared to take it. The great majority of evening classes are conducted by school boards; in 1965 over 80 per cent, involving 450 classes for 9,871 students. Normally, these classes meet two evenings a week from October to April.

Teachers in school board classes are required to have an Ontario teaching certificate and preference is given to teachers who have taken the summer course, "Teaching English as a Second Language," which has been offered since 1958 by the Department of Education and the Department of the Provincial Secretary and Citizenship. This whole programme is heavily subsidized by the federal government. It shares 90 per cent of the cost of school board classes with the provincial government, the local board assuming the remaining 10 per cent. A nominal fee of five dollars per year is normally charged by school boards for admission to their classes.

In a second category are the Citizenship Branch day classes, which operate five days a week from 8:30 a.m. to

2:30 p.m.; in 1965, there were classes of this kind in Hamilton, London, Sudbury and Toronto. The Citizenship Branch also operates some evening programmes, and some of a specialized nature—for example, at Ontario hospitals, the Workmen's Compensation Board Rehabilitation Centre, and in industry. In 1965, the number of day and evening classes sponsored by the Citizenship Branch was 59, with a combined enrolment of 1,043 students. Finally, in 1965, there were 224 "voluntary classes" enrolling 1,684 students; for these classes, which are sponsored by individual churches, clubs, and social agencies, there is no charge and the teachers are unpaid. The full cost of the Citizenship Branch classes is borne by the federal and provincial governments on a fifty-fifty basis.

There have been two significant developments during the past year. English has been recognized as an approved subject in the Canadian Vocational Training Programme 5 for unemployed persons; this means that lack of English is regarded in the same light as lack of a trade. Allowances are paid to those who enrol in language classes under the programme. Second, the Department of Education is now prepared to give special grants to school boards for the teaching of English to immigrant children.

Department of Reform Institutions

On March 31st, 1965, 1,281 boys and girls were in attendance at elementary and secondary school classes in the twelve Ontario Training Schools which are the responsibility of the Department of Reform Institutions. The majority of these young people were admitted to a training school through committal from a Family or Juvenile Court but a small percentage were admitted on application from a social welfare agency such as a Children's Aid Society. There are seven training schools for boys, five for girls. Three of the schools are operated by Roman Catholic religious orders but are fully subsidized by the department.

The maximum age limit is seventeen; there is no minimum (the 1965 enrolment included one child of eight), but legislation to make this twelve years of age is pending. Two-thirds of those in attendance in 1965 were thirteen, fourteen or fifteen. The school programme is a combination of the normal academic syllabus for the appropriate grade and vocational training of various types—sewing, cooking, "general domestic," machine shop, auto mechanics, barbering, etc. Each training school has different possibilities. Most students are at the Grade 7 to 9 level, and in the rare case where a student reaches Grade 12, an arrangement is made whereby the local secondary school grants the high school graduation diploma. The teachers are required to have the same qualifications as teachers in elementary and secondary schools, and supervision is provided by the local school inspector. A Department of Education official has over-all responsibility for the academic and vocational courses offered in the training schools. The department is also represented on the School Management Committee which, at each training school, supervises the school programme.

There is also an educational, or training, programme in the other institutions for which the department is responsible; in five reformatories, five industrial farms, and four minimum security training centres. All institutions accommodating inmates under the age of twenty have full-time academic teachers on the staff.

SUMMARY

An outline of the Ontario Educational System is provided in Chart 2 which identifies the major institutional

CHART 2 THE ONTARIO EDUCATIONAL SYSTEM 1965-66 (Numbers refer to full-time enrolment)

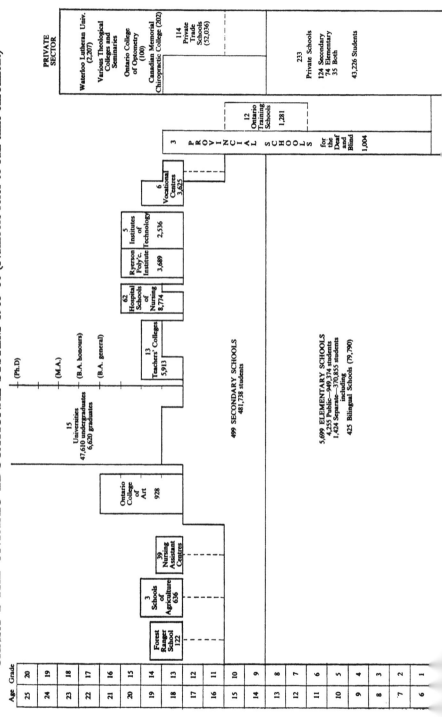

components of the system, relates each to the others by indicating the grade level required for admission, and records the full-time enrolment in 1965–6. The chart is an outline rather than a blueprint since the statistics are restricted to full-time enrolment and no reference is made to adult education. It will be noted that in four cases (Forest Ranger School, School of Agriculture, Nursing Assistants Centre, and the one-year courses at the Ontario Vocational Centres) the minimum academic admission requirement is Grade 10 but students are not accepted unless they are eighteen years of age. Most of the students at the Ontario Training Schools are in Grades 7 to 10 but the programme can extend both lower and higher.

The Development of the System, 1867-1966

In many respects the educational system of Ontario resembles the systems of other Canadian provinces and those of the American states; the chief exception has been Quebec, but under the Parent Commission arrangements the differences will be greatly reduced. Thus throughout North America there are features which can be said to be common to all educational systems; local school boards, a provincial or state department, kindergartens, hospital schools of nursing, apprenticeship programmes involving the co-operation of provincial or state Departments of Education and Labour, and many more. But each province and each state has certain features which are either unique or relatively unusual, and such features are of particular importance since they reflect the special interests or the special prejudices of the people of the province or state which have evolved in the course of decades or centuries. Because the unusual feature is the product of time, its rationale tends to be forgotten, and it is peculiarly subject to attack and criticism since its purpose often is not understood. The unusual feature can, of course, prove to be an anachronism; it may well have been relevant fifty or a hundred years ago but may now have been rendered obsolete by changing conditions and the discovery of more appropriate ways of dealing with the educational problem it was designed to resolve. But, for two reasons, it is the part of wisdom to think twice about the removal of a feature of an educational system which has characterized it for a long period of time. First, the recognition of its rationale may prove that it only appears to be an anachronism, that it does in fact still provide a solution to an educational problem that is not provided for in any other way. Second, the traditional feature may be woven into the fabric of the whole system in such a way that its removal, though justified on practical grounds, will disrupt related arrangements which are working well. One of the difficulties about education is that almost everything is related to everything else. It is like the children's pile of blocks: move or remove one block and all the others have to be realigned. And sometimes the removal of a block makes realignment impossible.

In order to understand the educational system of Ontario it is therefore essential to recognize its unique or distinctive features and to understand how they have come into being and are related to other elements of the system. There are at least seven features which require attention:

(1) separate schools extending to Grade 8 and in some cases to Grade 10 but not beyond;

(2) bilingual schools, with the course of study taught partly in English, partly in French, again to Grade 8 or 10;

(3) a five-year secondary school culminating in Grade 13;

(4) two quite separate types of undergraduate programmes in Arts and Science—three year general courses and four-year honours courses—both leading to the BA or BSc degree;

(5) entirely separate arrangements for the training of elementary and secondary school teachers;

(6) the relatively late (and consequently still incomplete) development of technical schools and technological institutes;

(7) the involvement of the Department of Education in an unusually wide range of adult education activities.

Since all of these matters are the consequence of gradual evolution over a long period of time and since they are related over time to the development of the system as a whole, I shall discuss them in the context of a general review of developments in the history of education in Ontario since 1867 in the six fields in which educational activity is normally divided: elementary education, secondary education, higher education, teaching training, vocational training, adult education. But first I shall describe briefly the position of education in Ontario in 1867.

EDUCATION IN ONTARIO IN 1867

In 1867 the Department of Education was engaged in all six of the broad areas into which educational activity is traditionally divided, but in two instances the involvement can only be described as nominal. Its claim that it was concerned with vocational training was based solely on the fact that a few subjects—bookkeeping, surveying, telegraphy—listed in the grammar school course of study might have been said to have been a direct preparation for future employment. The connection with higher education, signified by the inclusion of the universities' enrolment statistics in the Chief Superintendent's *Annual Report*, was based on the fact that, at this juncture, the Government paid legislative grants to universities and medical schools. These grants were discontinued in 1868, but in 1867 amounted to $22,650; $5,000 to Victoria and Queen's, $4,000 to Trinity, $3,000 to Regiopolis,[1] $2,000 to St. Michael's, $1,400 to Ottawa, and $750 each to the Toronto School of Medicine and the medical faculties of Queen's and Victoria. In the other four areas, however, the department was thoroughly engaged.

The Chief Superintendent's *Annual Report* was "of the Normal, Model, Grammar and Common Schools in Ontario" but it also included reference to the Education Museum, and to the department's services to free public libraries, both of which constituted an entry into the adult education field. The Education Museum, located in the Department of Education building and consisting of natural history specimens, casts of antique and modern sculpture, reproductions of the old masters, and models of agricultural "and other" implements, was intended primarily for the use of teachers, but it was open to the public at certain times, and in 1867 it was the closest thing to an art gallery and a museum that the province could boast. The mood of the department, which is what we are chiefly interested in, is caught in the following statement:

Nothing is more important than that an establishment designed especially to be the institution of the people at large—to provide for them teachers, apparatus, libraries, and every possible agency of instruction—should, in all its parts and appendages, be such as the people can contemplate with respect and satisfaction, and visit with pleasure and profit. While the schools have been established, and are so conducted as to leave nothing to be desired in regard to their character and efficiency, the accompanying agencies for the agreeable and substantial improvement of all classes of students and pupils, and for the useful entertainment of numerous visitors from various parts of the country, as well as many from abroad, have been rendered as attractive and complete as the limited means furnished would permit. Such are the objects of the Educational Museum.[2]

Another agency of the department, the Educational

Depository, had been established in 1851 to provide equipment—maps, globes, apparatus, "object lessons," books—essentially at cost, to the schools, but it, too, served the general public. In 1867, 5,426 volumes "procured by the Education Department from publishers in both Europe and America at as low a price as possible" were supplied to free public libraries (raising the total since the introduction of the service to 224,647) while 8,722 were supplied to the mechanics institutes.

The department was involved at this time in an even more unexpected area—the reporting of meteorological observations. The Grammar School Act of 1865 had authorized the establishment of weather stations at Barrie, Belleville, Cornwall, Goderich, Hamilton, Pembroke, Peterborough, Simcoe, Stratford, and Windsor, at which observations were taken three times daily (7:00 am, 1:00 pm, 9:00 pm) by official observers, often assisted by "some diligent pupil." The reports were published in the *Journal of Education*, a monthly which the department also found time to publish, one of the five thousand copies being placed in the hands of every trustee, local superintendent, county

TABLE 2

The Ontario Educational System, 1867

Type of school	Number of schools	Number of students
Common schools	4,422	382,719
Separate schools	161	18,924
Model schools (attached to normal school)	2	547
Grammar schools	102	5,696
Private schools & academies (including 16 "colleges")	312	6,743
Normal school (2 sessions)	1	253
TOTAL	5,000	414,882

clerk, and county treasurer. One explanation for the fatness of the Chief Superintendent's *Annual Report* for 1867 was the inclusion of the year's programme and an analysis of this whole operation.

Most of the over three hundred pages of the report were, however, concerned with the department's work in the field of elementary and secondary schooling and teacher training. This was an enterprise involving over 400,000 students in exactly 5,000 schools (see Table 2).

This, then, was the educational system upon which the developments of the past century have been based, comprised of many elementary and secondary schools, a single teacher training institution, a collection of independent universities and colleges, and a number of adult education services.

ELEMENTARY EDUCATION

There is general agreement that Egerton Ryerson was the effective creator of the Ontario educational system. It is true that a surprising number of schools and colleges of various kinds were in operation at the time of his appointment as Chief Superintendent in 1844, and one can, with the exercise of some ingenuity, detect in the arrangements then in force the basic ingredients of the present organization; central department, local school boards, separate schools, legislative grants, local taxes, and so forth. But it was Ryerson who organized, related, and defined the basic elements and who provided the philosophic ideas which gave the developing system cohesion, inner consistency, and purposefulness.

Ryerson's extraordinary success, which can be readily appreciated by comparing the situation when he assumed office in 1846 with the situation in 1876 when he retired, was due in considerable measure to the fact that he was a political realist. He knew that Utopia cannot be achieved by legislative fiat, and that if the people of Ontario were to provide the funds needed to support a proper educational system they must be convinced of its value and, just as importantly, of its attainability. Hence his constant efforts to explain to the people of the province, and not merely to the legislators, what his plans were and why they adopted the form they did. He also knew that first things have to come first, that one builds a house from the ground up and not in defiance of the laws of gravity. Hence the concentration of his efforts at the outset on the common (i.e., elementary) schools and on the related matter of training for common school teachers. This was not only the most obvious task, it was also the most difficult, partly because its accomplishment would imply the acceptance of certain principles, which once adopted for one type of schooling would be acceptable in others without too much question. It required twenty years of steady effort to build the ground floor, but by 1867 the job was essentially done. Ryerson devoted the remaining ten years of his superintendency to the organization of the secondary schools, and by 1876 the plan for the second level of the system was complete. By then, however, his time had run out. It is an interesting speculation to wonder what other floors Ryerson would have constructed if he had continued in full vigour until, say, 1890.

The fact that the elementary school system had been thoroughly organized by 1867 is one reason for there being less to say about developments in this area between 1867 and 1966 than about developments in, for example, the secondary schools and teacher training. But there are two other reasons. One is that the elementary is by nature the most static of the educational levels; the curriculum is basically the three Rs, which change very little from decade to decade, and the main problem is to see that it is made available under proper conditions—good teachers, reasonable equipment—to all children. There are, of course, children who require special attention, children for whom for any of a number of reasons the normal course of study is inadequate or inappropriate, and we shall, therefore, have something to say about Ontario's record in providing for the needs of this group.

The second reason for brevity in this section is that the two components of elementary schooling in Ontario that are distinctive—separate schools and bilingual schools— are subjects which have been thoroughly examined in recent studies. Anyone concerned with the separate school question must turn to the chapter on Ontario in C. B. Sissons' *Church and State in Canadian Education*, to Franklin Walker's twin studies, *Catholic Education and Politics in Upper Canada* and *Catholic Education and Politics in Ontario*, and to the lengthy appendix to the *Report of the Royal Commission on Education in Ontario* (1950) entitled "A History of the Roman Catholic Separate School Controversy." Similarly those interested in the bilingual school issue will wish to consult Chapter XVI of the Royal Commission Report, "History of the French Languages in the Public Schools of Ontario," and the chapters on Ontario in C. B. Sissons' *Bilingual Schools in Canada*, as well as the works mentioned above. Neither topic lends itself to easy summation and none will be attempted here. I shall confine my comments to the consequences for the system as a whole of the inclusion of separate and bilingual schools as integral parts of the system.

Separate Schools and Bilingual Schools

It is important to recognize that separate and bilingual schools are not synonymous. The great majority of separate schools are indistinguishable from the public schools so far as language of instruction is concerned, and a good proportion of the bilingual schools are public. To the extent that the separate and the bilingual schools can be said to constitute a problem for the system as a whole, there are two problems, not one.

It is possible that a comparison of the qualifications of the teachers and of the physical facilities provided in the two types of publicly-supported elementary schools would lead to the conclusion that a better education was provided in the public schools; the public schools have, on the average, greater financial resources to draw upon and can therefore pay higher salaries and provide more and better equipment. Such a conclusion, however, would have little meaning since it would ignore both the personality of the individual teacher and the differences which unquestionably exist between particular schools. If one compares the qualifications of the teachers or the adequacy of the physical facilities provided in the schools of a metropolitan area like Toronto with those in, let us say, the Muskoka District, one finds striking contrasts, but these apply whether the comparison is between the public schools of the two areas or the separate schools of the two areas or both. Furthermore, there is no inevitable cause-and-effect relationship between professional or academic qualifications and actual performance in the classroom. Some excellent teachers have "poor" qualifications and some poor teachers are "well" qualified. At the elementary school level in particular, teaching is too intimate a matter to justify any conclusion which is based on evidence that leaves out of account the personal or human factor.

The most important consequence of the inclusion of the separate schools as an integral part of the Ontario educational system has been the tendency for this to inhibit any fundamental restructuring of the system as a whole. This was dramatically illustrated fifteen years ago in the *Report*

of the Royal Commission on Education in Ontario, 1950.
The Commission (twenty members) sat for five years
and produced both majority and minority reports, as well
as a number of memoranda recording the dissent of individual members to particular recommendations of the
majority report. One commissioner found it impossible
to sign either report. While there were a number of areas
where differences of opinion were sufficiently great to render
compromise difficult (the training of elementary school
teachers, for example), the main cause of disagreement
was with respect to the proposal that the jurisdiction of
separate schools end at Grade 6. All members of the Commission were of the view that the school system should
adopt the 6:4:3 plan—six grades of elementary education,
followed by four grades of secondary, followed by three
grades of what was to be called junior college—but the
majority insisted that the separate schools should be confined to elementary education, whereas the minority, all
of whom were separate school supporters, insisted that both
elementary and secondary education as thus defined should
be provided in denominational schools. And that effectively
was that. Many of the Commission's recommendations have
been adopted, but none which has involved any alteration
of the system's basic structure. But, as the *Report of the
Royal Commission of Inquiry on Education in the Province
of Quebec* has recently demonstrated, the key to fundamental change usually lies in basic restructuring.

The existence of two types of elementary school has
unquestionably had the effect of dividing those interested in
what are essentially the same problems into different groups.
Thus in Ontario there are associations for separate school
trustees and also associations for public school trustees;
and there are associations of separate school teachers and
associations of public school teachers. It is true that in both
cases there are organizations which embrace the separate

associations—the Ontario School Trustees' Council and the Ontario Teachers' Federation—but it is also true that the concern of most trustees and teachers is less with provincial than with local matters. Trustees tend to be separate school trustees or public school trustees rather than just trustees, and teachers too often see too little of their colleagues in the "other" camp.

It could also be argued that since the basic qualification for the teacher in the bilingual schools is technically lower (Grade 12) than that required for the English-speaking schools (Grade 13), their existence lowers the standard of teacher training in the province. It is possible, however, that the requirement of fluency in two languages to the Grade 12 level is as demanding as competence in one to the Grade 13 level. In any event, the basic reason that a Second Class Certificate is accepted for the teacher in the bilingual schools is the shortage of available candidates. The provision of higher salaries in the bilingual schools would reduce the problem but it would not permanently remove it.

The bilingual schools are a method of dealing with the special problems posed by the educational needs of the French-speaking communities of Ontario; they are not the cause of the problem but an attempt to do something about it. The problem itself is essentially sociological; the plight of a linguistic minority whose members require mastery of one language for the maintenance and development of their cultural tradition, and mastery of a second for reasons that are economic and circumstantial. The task that faces the bilingual schools is a difficult one; to develop effective bilingualism by the end of Grade 8, or at best by Grade 10, for at that point the student must proceed, if he is to remain in the public school system, to a secondary school where the great bulk of the instruction, including all instruction in science and technology, is available only in English. If it is evident that the bilingual schools cannot achieve this result, a way must surely be found to provide more effectively in the public high schools for the French-speaking student so that his education can be continued.

It is worth noting that the establishment of both separate and bilingual schools can be regarded as simply two, albeit the most important, among many steps adopted by the province to provide appropriate educational arrangements for *all* its young people. The province has, on the whole, a very good record of concerning itself with the needs of the child, or the adult, who requires a special educational service. Schools for the deaf and the blind were opened in 1870 and 1871, kindergartens were authorized in the early 1880s, and industrial schools for "delinquent" boys and girls were established in the late 1880s. Special classes for the slow learners were introduced in the public school system in 1910. In 1921, the physically handicapped were cared for with the establishment of sight-saving classes for the near blind, hard-of-hearing classes for the partially deaf, and speech correction classes for children with speech impediments. The Department of Education, in 1901, initiated a scheme by which travelling libraries were sent to mining and forestry camps in Northern Ontario and to "groups of taxpayers living in hamlets."[3] In 1928 schooling was brought to children in the remote areas south of James Bay by way of the railway car.[4] This is not to say, of course, that a large proportion of the handicapped or the geographically disadvantaged children, or adults, of the province have been well provided for; all such arrangements are normally dependent for their actual implementation upon the willingness of the child's parent and/or the local community to take advantage of what the central authority is prepared to offer, and unfortunately this willingness is not always displayed. But the fact that special services have not been provided for all children in the province who need them does not cancel out the fact that the Department of Education has over the years shown considerable imagination and energy in making such services available to many of them.

SECONDARY EDUCATION

The Evolution of Grade 13

In 1867 the organization of secondary education in Ontario was still very much in a formative stage. Despite Grammar School Acts of 1807, 1819, 1839, 1853, 1855, and 1865, the relation of the individual school to either the central department on the one hand or the local municipality on the other was loose and its financial position insecure. Municipalities could provide for the support of the local grammar school by taxation based on the property tax, but they were not required to do so. Many of the students were elementary school pupils whom the grammar schools enrolled as a means of increasing their income; the students paid a tuition fee and the grant from the Grammar School Fund administered by the superintendent was based on total enrolment. The right of girls to attend grammar schools as regular students was not conclusively established until 1869.

The 1871 Act to Improve the Common and Grammar Schools of Ontario changed the situation completely. A clear-cut division was now made between elementary schooling—assigned exclusively to the "public schools" as the common schools were henceforth to be called—and secondary education, which would be carried on in collegiate institutes and in high schools. To be admitted to either a collegiate institute or a high school, the pupil had to pass the entrance examination, based on the work of the final grade of the public school. The municipality was required to provide the local share of the cost of both types of secondary schools from the property tax. The main function of the high school was to offer a general course which would concentrate upon "the higher branches of an English and Commercial Education, including the Natural Sciences and with special reference to Agriculture." The collegiate institutes, which were seen as "the proper link between the Public School and the University," were to concentrate on the subjects required for university matriculation, notably the ancient and modern languages. High schools were, however, permitted to offer Latin, Greek, French, and German to children "whose parents or guardian may desire it." Apparently, many parents did so desire. Also, a great many high school principals encouraged students to take the collegiate subjects in order to change the status of the school to that of a collegiate institute so that it would qualify for the special $750 annual grant which a collegiate institute was entitled to receive. One way or other, the intended differentiation between the two types of secondary school did not materialize. By 1890 both the English and the Classical courses were being offered in both high schools and collegiate institutes and the original qualifications for the status of collegiate institute—a minimum of four masters and a minimum of sixty students enrolled in classics—had been replaced by the requirement that there be four members of the staff who were "specialists" in either English, classics, moderns, mathematics, or natural science. As we shall see this requirement had an important influence on the development of honours courses at the universities and on the arrangements for the training of secondary school teachers.

Courses of study for both the classical and general courses were announced in August 1871 and came into operation in January 1872. There were to be four forms (or grades). In 1876 the term, "Lower School," was applied to the work of the first two forms, and "Upper School," to the final two forms, and the student was required to pass an examination, the "Intermediate," in order to be admitted to Upper

School. The work of Form III, the first of the two Upper School years, was that of junior matriculation, required for admission to the first year of a university course. Students in Form IV were preparing for senior matriculation which admitted to the second year of certain university courses.[5] At this stage, Ontario could be said to have had either a three-year high school which, among other things, was preparatory to a four-year university course or a four-year high school preparatory to a three-year university course. The senior matriculation year, which permitted the student to do a year of university work at the local secondary school, can be regarded as an anticipation of the junior college plan introduced in the United States twenty-five years later.

In the mid-1890s, the junior matriculation examinations were divided into two parts. By this time (as will be described in a following section[6]), most of the Ontario universities had developed the honours as well as the general BA course, and junior matriculation with honours was beginning to be required in some subjects for admission to certain honours courses. Only one examination was set in junior matriculation Part I, but both honours and pass papers were set in some subjects of Part II. Parts I and II, furthermore, were to be written at different times. This led in 1904 to the introduction of "Middle School" to which Part I of junior matriculation was assigned, Part II of junior matriculation and senior matriculation constituting the work of Upper School. By 1913 Lower, Middle, and Upper School were each two years in length, and Ontario had a six-year high school. But in 1921, chiefly to encourage students who where not planning to go to university to complete the high school course, Upper School was reduced to a single year. This resulted in the five-year high school which Ontario continues to maintain. Throughout the 1920s all the Ontario universities continued to accept junior matriculants into the first year and senior matriculants into the second, but in 1931 the University of Toronto decided to require senior matriculation of all applicants. The Toronto general BA now became officially a three-year course from senior matriculation, the honours BA a four-year course from senior matriculation. Throughout the 1930s and 1940s the other Ontario universities continued to admit some students with junior matriculation, but increasingly the Toronto model was imitated and by the mid-1950s the practice of requiring senior matriculation was general. In September 1965 less than one thousand of the over seventeen thousand freshmen who entered Ontario universities were admitted with junior matriculation to what had come to be called a Preliminary, or Qualifying, Year.

Vocational Education in the Secondary School

What has been said so far may give the impression that secondary education in Ontario since the 1870s has been primarily a matter of providing an academic course for students who intend to go on to university. Nothing could be further from the truth.

The significant fact about the failure of the collegiate institute and the high school to develop as different kinds of secondary school is not that the high schools assumed the task of teaching the classical course but that the collegiates assumed the task of teaching the general course. Conceivably, a better university preparatory course would have developed if certain schools had concentrated on this single task, and conceivably a better general course with the technological and vocational orientation implied by the phrase, "an English and Commercial Course, including the Natural Sciences and with special reference to Agriculture," would have been developed if this had been the sole concern of the high school. But such an arrangement would certainly have divided the secondary school population into two very distinct groups, a relatively small academically gifted *élite*, including no doubt a sizable proportion of the non-academically gifted from the upper bracket of the socio-economic scale, and the rest who, no doubt, would include a sizable number of the academically gifted from the lower bracket of that same scale. It is also likely that the original plan would have led to the existence of two different types of secondary school teacher, those concerned with the scholars and those concerned with the masses. Neither of such outcomes could be said to be particularly in harmony with the North American tradition.

It is also worth noting that Ontario's actual experience with secondary schools which concentrate upon an *élite* group does not suggest that the practice should have been universally adopted. There have always been a small number of private boarding schools in Ontario, and since 1910 one day school, the University of Toronto Schools, which, in a sense, have adopted the posture of the collegiate institutes as originally conceived. There have been over the years many distinguished graduates of each of these schools, and UTS in particular has always occupied a position of consistent prominence on the university scholarship lists. But it is not at all clear that the contribution of the graduates of these schools to the scientific, artistic, and intellectual development of Canada is superior to that of, for example, the graduates of Jarvis Collegiate Institute in Toronto or of Lisgar Collegiate Institute in Ottawa. And despite the evidence documenting the influence of Upper Canada College graduates on the economic life of Canada presented in John Porter's recently published *The Vertical Mosaic*, it is not even clear that the educational merits of the *élite* school are responsible for such influence, even in the world of finance. As Professor Porter makes clear, academic programme is one thing, the advantages of knowing the right people quite another, and any true comparison of the relative merits of the two kinds of school would have to rule out of consideration the irrelevancies represented by the latter. No one has ever demonstrated any causal connection between the academic programme offered at Upper Canada College and the subsequent careers of its graduates.

It would, however, be misleading to suggest that the general course provided in the Ontario secondary schools either in the 1870s or in any decade since has been an unqualified success. The tendency has been to give first priority to what is needed to render efficient the classical or, as it came to be called, the academic course, and far too many students, whose interest and talents called for more practical subjects, have wrestled with Latin, French, and trigonometry. But the explanation for such misdirection and for the preponderant concern for the university preparatory course is to be found in the realm of social attitudes. In Ontario, as in many other places, it has always been difficult to convince parents that the university preparatory course is not the most suitable choice for their particular son or daughter.

Courses other than the university preparatory have always been available and the record of the Department of Education in providing alternatives has been reasonably good: commercial departments were authorized in 1891, manual training and household science were introduced at the turn of the century, and in 1897, high school boards were empowered to establish technical schools. By 1904 manual training, household science, art, and agriculture were listed as secondary school courses, along with university matriculation, teachers' non-professional certificate, commercial, and general. In 1907, agriculture, which had been flirted with as a secondary school subject since 1847, was at long last placed on a solid footing, a two-year course taught by graduates of the Ontario Agricultural College being introduced at the Essex High School near Windsor and at the

collegiate institutes at Lindsay, Perth, Morrisburg, Colling-
wood, and Galt. In 1911 the department appointed a Director of Elementary Agricultural Education.

In 1901 the department had appointed Albert Leake
Director of Manual Training and Technical Education but,
as he gloomily pointed out in his report to the Minister
(1905), not much was being accomplished in this area.[7]
Noting that, in addition to his own annual reports there had
been special reports on technical education in 1871, 1889,
1899 (two), 1900, 1901, and 1902, he commented that
none of these had received the attention it deserved. He
presented his 1905 report "with the hope that it [would]
meet a better fate and that neither apathy, indifference nor
mistaken economy will prevent earnest consideration of the
suggestions made." Leake's fifth report received no better
fate than its predecessors, but a change did occur as the
result of yet another report, submitted in 1910. This was
Education for Industrial Purposes prepared by John Seath,
who had been appointed Chief Director of Education in
1906, and who had been commissioned in 1909 to report
upon and submit a plan for a practicable system of technical
education for Ontario. Most of his recommendations were
implemented in the Industrial Education Act of 1911,
which, among other things, provided for the appointment
of a Director of Industrial and Technical Education and for
the establishment and support of both day and evening technical and industrial schools.

The first Director was F. W. Merchant who spent a full
year studying vocational education in Europe and North
America before actually assuming his duties in September
1913. Despite the failure of the federal government to act
until 1919 upon its proposal (of 1913) to provide substantial financial support for provincial programmes of vocational training, and despite the slow-down and disruption
of the new programme that was the inevitable consequence

of the war years, the progress made during Merchant's ten years as Director was extraordinary. By 1923 there were sixteen vocational schools in the province with a full-time enrolment of nearly 7,000 and a part-time enrolment of just under 1,000. Over forty branches of instruction—among them plumbing, printing and bookbinding, industrial design, horology, millinery, and power plant operation—were available at one or more schools. In addition 33,000 persons were enrolled in the evening vocational classes offered in these sixteen vocational schools and in the thirty-four collegiate institutes or high schools which had developed vocational courses; as an example, 508 evening students were taking printing and bookbinding in thirty different schools.

The expansion of vocational training continued throughout the 1920s and 1930s. By 1928 there were forty-two day vocational schools and a full-time enrolment of 21,604, and by 1938 there were sixty-two with an enrolment of 36,481. The movement was encouraged both by the raising of the upper age of compulsory schooling in 1919 from fourteen to sixteen and by the passing of the Apprenticeship Act of 1928 which placed responsibility for the academic portion of the apprentice's programme upon the technical schools. Enrolment increased rather than decreased during the Depression.

It is important to recognize that this whole development of vocational training took place *within* the framework of the secondary school. *There was no parallel development of vocational training at the post-secondary level until after the Second World War.* It could be argued that the secondary school vocational programme introduced and implemented by Seath and Merchant was too successful and that much more of it should have been developed outside and beyond the high school, but certainly during this period neither the Department of Education nor the school boards of the province could be accused of apathy, indifference, or mistaken economy in their attitude towards technical education.

Departmental Examinations

One other matter deserves comment in reviewing the development of secondary education in Ontario between 1867 and 1965—that is, the heavy emphasis that has been placed upon departmental examinations as a means of maintaining, or raising, standards. Since departmental examinations are an example of central rather than local control, the "examination incubus" has often been regarded as the triumph of bureaucracy over the individual. The case was classically put by E. G. Savage, an English inspector who spent six months on exchange with the Ontario Department of Education in 1926:

Centralisation is complete in Ontario. The Department of Education regulates the subjects to be taken, the length of time for which some of them at least may be studied and the year in which they shall be studied; it issues syllabuses in each subject and prescribes text-books which must be used. Finally it examines the product. Little or nothing is left to the initiative of the Principal or of the teachers. All that is necessary is for the teachers, all trained in the same professional school, to follow the syllabus and the text-book, and to see that the facts enshrined therein are known. This is what is, for the most part, done. Pupils of the most ordinary intelligence can then scarcely fail to pass the examiners. Unhappily the adventurer electing to stray afield will receive no credit for his adventures and indeed places himself under a handicap by his wanderings.
There are historical reasons for this high degree of centralisation. It may well have been suited to earlier days when schools were small, and before a tradition of scholarship had been built up. Unhappily it prevents such a tradition from becoming established. It obviously still has its value in the case of small schools with two or three teachers, not perhaps highly qualified in any sense. For these the departmental requirements afford a crutch without which the school would be indeed a lame affair. In

this sense the minutely regulated curriculum serves a useful purpose in that it makes possible the establishment of secondary schools in very small places and guarantees that they shall reach a minimum standard. The unfortunate results are that the minimum tends to become the normal and the able teachers in the large Collegiate Institutes in the big cities find the crutch a handicap. It prevents them from going at more than a walking pace, and entirely prevents excursions off the common track. The Collegiate Institutes number on their staffs many teachers of real ability, artists in their various subjects who are capable of creative work, but these find little scope for their abilities and in the course of a few years they tend to become reconciled to the dull round and settle down to become cogs in the machine. There is complete uniformity of method, and at length comes a lack of interest in other methods and in other text-books. The machine works but it has a tendency to get into ruts from which the overworked officers of the department have no time to spare from routine work to get it out.[8]

Certainly in 1926 departmental examinations had a familiar ring for the student who made his way to the end of the secondary school course. He could have been required to write four complete sets—the High School Entrance Examination and the examinations at the end of each of Lower, Middle, and Upper School. By 1926, however, the recommendation of the elementary school principal could be accepted in lieu of the High School Entrance Examination and two-thirds of the students who obtained entrance that year were admitted on this basis. An even higher percentage were granted standing for Lower School on the teacher's recommendation. In 1932 the principle of recommendation was extended to Middle School (or junior matriculation). In 1935 it became possible to be recommended for Upper School (or senior matriculation) papers, and for the next four years it was theoretically possible to enter university without ever having faced an external examination. In 1940 the senior matriculation examinations became again obligatory for all students, although for a time there

were special wartime provisions for those who enlisted or
worked on farms. In 1937 the examination for Lower
School was withdrawn, in 1940 the examination for junior
matriculation, and in 1949 the examination for high school
entrance. Since 1950 the only departmental examinations
have been those for senior matriculation. In 1964–5, following a recommendation of the Grade 13 Study Committee
of 1964, the teacher's term mark was assigned a value of
25 per cent in the final standing assigned the student at
senior matriculation, and in 1965–6, this was raised to 35
per cent.

In April 1966, it was announced that departmental
examinations for senior matriculation would be withdrawn
at the end of the 1967–8 school year. Thereafter, the senior
matriculation examination in each subject will be set and
marked by the staff of each secondary school. The Department of Education will continue to administer aptitude and
achievement tests of an objective nature, a service it began
to provide in 1959.

Clearly the practice has changed since Savage's visit—
perhaps his was a report which did receive the attention it
deserved. Certainly this can be said of the *Report of the
Grade 13 Study Committee* which recommended both the
introduction of the teacher's term mark into the determina-
tion of final standing and the eventual abolition of the
departmental examinations. The use of the teacher's term
mark was designed partly to reduce the pressure on the
student; at the point where the passing of the senior matriculation examinations was the sole criterion for admission to
university, these tests became of particularly crucial importance to the student, with everything depending on his
performance in a series of single 2½-hour examinations,
written under conditions he had never faced before. With
the introduction of the term mark he was judged partly on
the basis of his year's work. But the main objective of the

Grade 13 Study Committee in recommending that the teacher's mark be taken into account was to correct the situation of which Savage complained. If the examination paper is not the sole criterion for determining the student's standing, the able teacher can go at more than a walking pace and he can take excursions off the common track.

Finally it should be noted that Savage was accurate in his assessment of how the departmental examination had come to occupy such a prominent position in the educational system of Ontario. In 1867 there were 102 secondary schools; by 1926 the number had risen to 442 and over 200 of these were continuation schools with one or two teachers. In these latter schools at least there were many teachers in 1926 who did need a crutch.

Today the movement to consolidate small rural schools into large district high schools is well advanced, and this argument in favour of retaining departmental examinations has lost its force.

HIGHER EDUCATION

Government Support for Higher Education

It has already been noted that a number of universities and colleges received legislative grants in 1867, specifically Queen's, Victoria, Trinity, Ottawa, Regiopolis, and St. Michael's.[9] It may not have been noticed that the University of Toronto was not among them, despite the fact that it was officially the Provincial University. Toronto was, however, the beneficiary of an endowment of approximately 225,000 acres of Crown land which had been authorized in 1798, and in 1867 the income it received from this source and from tuition fees was sufficient to its needs. The other universities had been attempting to obtain a share of this endowment since their respective establishments and the grants they had been receiving from the Legislature could be described either as consolation prizes or as sops to the legislative conscience. The argument against providing them with a share of the endowment was that as denominational institutions they were not eligible to benefit from a fund which had been established for the advancement of higher education for all the people of the province. The Provincial University, it was argued, was open to all, and a denomination's decision to establish its own university was one for which it must bear full financial responsibility. It was precisely this line of reasoning which led the Government in 1867 to announce that no further grants would be made to denominational institutions after 1868.

The Government's support for higher education during the next quarter century was confined to those institutions which it itself established and controlled—the School of Technology, which was soon renamed the School of Practical Science, and the Ontario College of Agriculture. The former, which opened in Toronto in 1872, was, from 1875, closely associated with the University of Toronto. Its permanent building was constructed on the University of Toronto campus in 1878 and several of its professors were also members of the University College staff. In 1889 the School of Practical Science entered into affiliation with the University of Toronto and its students began to receive University of Toronto degrees. But until 1906, when it became the Faculty of Applied Science and Engineering, its budget was quite separate from the university's and control was exercised from Queen's Park. Since the Ontario Agricultural College, which was established in 1874, was located sixty miles away at Guelph, its association with the University of Toronto was not nearly so close, but in 1888 it also entered into affiliation and for the next seventy-five years its graduates also received University of Toronto degrees. Again the budget was quite separate.

From the outset until the establishment of the University of Guelph on July 1, 1964, responsibility for the Ontario Agricultural College rested primarily with the Department of Agriculture.

The establishment of these two professional schools in the early 1870s was a recognition of the growing importance of science and technology, and it was this same awareness which convinced the University of Toronto in 1883 that the time had come when its endowment income was no longer sufficient to enable it to fulfil its provincial role. This income was adequate to the needs of an institution offering the traditional liberal arts subjects, but not for one which was expected to have proper laboratories for teaching and research in the physical and natural sciences. The proposal that it should receive an annual grant led to a general discussion of the university situation in the province in which all institutions participated, for the problem of how to meet the costs of science was also of concern to Ottawa, Queen's, Victoria, Trinity, and the others. Out of these deliberations evolved the University of Toronto Federation Act of 1887.

This act enabled a university entering into federation with the University of Toronto to provide for all the needs of its arts and science students at relatively little cost to itself. The instruction it would henceforth provide would be confined to theology, which it would carry on independently and within the framework of its own degree-granting powers, and to six subjects in arts—classics, English, French, German, Orientals, and ethics—which it would offer in the context of an arts college within the University of Toronto's Faculty of Arts. The university would assume responsibility for all other instruction offered in the Faculty of Arts including the expensive area of science, as well as in all professional fields except theology. Victoria University's decision to accept this arrangement in 1890, one which necessitated a move from Cobourg to Toronto, transformed this ingenious theory into a practical fact. Trinity University followed suit in 1904 and St. Michael's College, which had entered federation on a somewhat different basis in 1887, attained equivalent status in 1910.[10]

When the University of Toronto for its part agreed to the federation plan it assumed that it would receive from the Government an annual grant to enable it to finance the additional costs of its necessarily much expanded operation, but it was not until 1901 that any grant in support of its teaching departments was forthcoming, and not until 1907 that the annual support could be described as substantial. In the meantime, the Government had begun in 1893 to provide grants in support of the Kingston School of Mines, which was in effect—and in 1916 became in fact—Queen's University's Faculty of Applied Science. In 1909 an additional grant was made to Queen's for the Faculty of Education which, at the request of the Government, it had agreed to establish, and in 1913, the year after Queen's had removed its denominational ties, there was a grant for general purposes. Commencing in 1915, Western University at London, also by this time an undenominational institution, began to receive grants for general purposes—for three years before this it had received a grant for its Institute of Public Health. The role of Queen's and Western as public institutions in the eastern and western parts of Southern Ontario was emphasized by a Royal Commission in 1920, and their "right" to an annual maintenance grant was confirmed.[11] In 1939 the amount was $250,000 for Queen's, and $260,000 for Western. Toronto's grant in the same year for operating purposes was $1,316,000.[12] No grants were made to the only two other universities which were active at this time—McMaster and Ottawa—both of which were denominationally controlled.

Commencing in 1947, when a grant was made to the University of Ottawa for its Faculty of Medicine, the

Government began to develop the policy of providing funds in support of both capital and operating expenses to all universities of the province not under denominational control. In three instances—Ottawa, McMaster, and Windsor (then Assumption)—the grant for a number of years was made to a university which was still under denominational control but specifically for the support of work (medicine, engineering, pure science) which could under no stretch of the imagination be described as "denominational" —in the case of McMaster and Assumption such grants were actually made to a separately governed affiliate. All three of these institutions are now undenominational and grants are made for general purposes.

Federation and Affiliation

The sixteen degree-granting institutions which are operating in the province today are in striking contrast to the five which existed in 1939, but the expansion is in one sense less dramatic than at first appears. Four of the new universities existed in embryo form *within* the five universities of 1939: the University of Guelph as the Ontario Agricultural College, affiliated with the University of Toronto; the University of Windsor as Assumption College, an affiliate of the University of Western Ontario; and the University of Waterloo and Waterloo Lutheran University as Waterloo College, another Western affiliate. Two others are outgrowths of institutions active in 1939 but not at that time empowered to grant degrees—Osgoode Hall Law School established in 1889 and Laurentian University, one of whose federating elements originated in the Collège du Sacré-Cœur, established at Sudbury in 1913. Of the universities created since 1939 only two, Brock and Trent, began *de novo* as chartered institutions; Carleton received a charter in 1952 after a decade of operation, initially as an institution for part-time students, Lakehead (1962) evolved from an institute of technology established by the Department of Education in 1948, while for the first four years of York's existence it operated as an affiliate of the University of Toronto. In Ontario, universities tend to develop by subdivision and transformation rather than by spontaneous combustion.

In a sense this is an indirect consequence of the Federation Act of 1887 which demonstrated both the advantages and the feasibility of institutional co-operation. No other Ontario university has adopted Toronto's particular type of federated structure but almost all have experimented with some kind of federation or affiliation arrangement or, as is the case with three of the recently established institutions (Brock, Trent, and York), are in the process of developing a college system. The exceptions are Carleton, Lakehead, and Osgoode Hall.

Thus both McMaster and Windsor (when Assumption) adopted the stratagem of creating an undenominational affiliate (Hamilton College 1948–57, Essex College 1956–62) with which the university could share instructional responsibility in an attempt to resolve the financial problem faced by a denominational institution which, because it is denominational, cannot qualify for provincial funds. The University of Waterloo owes its origin to a similar attempt; in 1957 Waterloo College, a Lutheran controlled affiliate of the University of Western Ontario, arranged for the establishment of the independently controlled Waterloo College Associated Faculties, which would be eligible for provincial grants. The Associated Faculties would provide courses in science and engineering while Waterloo, severing its ties with Western, would offer arts and theology. This scheme did not work out, but it did have the effect of creating the University of Waterloo (from the Waterloo College Associated Faculties) and Waterloo Lutheran University (from Waterloo College). The University of Waterloo has subsequently adopted a federated structure which approximates the Toronto model: the University of St. Jerome's College, a Roman Catholic institution which dates back to 1864, is a federated university, and there are three affiliated colleges—Conrad Grabel (Mennonite), Renison (Anglican), St. Paul's (United Church)—which also provide some instruction in arts.

As has been noted, both Assumption and Waterloo Colleges, the forerunners of Windsor and Waterloo Lutheran, were, at the time they received charters, affiliates of the University of Western Ontario, associations which began in 1919 and 1925, respectively. The Western plan differed from Toronto's in that the affiliate college taught all the subjects in the arts and science curriculum; the students at Waterloo and Windsor wrote the same examinations as the students at London and received the Western degree. Western also has three affiliated colleges on its own campus— Brescia, a Roman Catholic college for women; King's College, a Roman Catholic college for men; and Huron, an Anglican college—which offer undergraduate work at both general and honours level in co-operation with the university's Faculty of Arts and Science.

We have also noted the unusual alliance of institutions at Guelph; the Ontario Agricultural College and the Ontario Veterinary College, each for many years separately affiliated with the University of Toronto, and the Macdonald Institute, a division of the Ontario Agricultural College. Until the establishment of the University of Guelph in 1964 all three were financed by the Department of Agriculture, and from 1961 to 1964 were called the Federated Colleges of the Department of Agriculture. Still to be mentioned are the University of Ottawa, which since 1932 has had in St. Patrick's an associated college which offers courses leading to a number of University of Ottawa degrees parallel to those of the university itself, and which is autonomous in administration and financial matters; Queen's University at Kingston, which has in the Queen's Theological College an affiliate; and Laurentian University of Sudbury, with which are federated (not affiliated) Huntington University (United Church), l'Université de Sudbury (Roman Catholic), and Thorneloe University (Anglican). Each of the federated universities offers courses in philosophy and religious knowledge within Laurentian's undergraduate programme in arts and science.

The Development of Honours Courses

While it is relatively easy to document Ontario's extensive experience with various kinds of affiliation and federation arrangements and to relate this to the ease with which new universities have been established in recent years, it is very difficult to establish that the University of Toronto had any necessary influence on these events. The developments at Western Ontario, Laurentian, and elsewhere might very well have happened even if the Federation Act had never been passed. However, there is no doubt whatsoever that another University of Toronto movement of the 1880s had a direct, powerful, and continuing influence on higher education in the province and on teacher training and secondary school education as well. This was the development of honours courses in arts and science.

The beginnings of the honours course system, which is such a distinctive feature of the Ontario educational scene, can be traced to the late 1850s when students in the BA course at the University of Toronto were permitted to drop certain courses if they were pursuing honours in certain others. For some years Toronto, Trinity, and several other Canadian institutions had been awarding prizes in particular subjects for students who wrote special examinations on work not prescribed in the regular course. The "candidate for honours" simply did additional work. What was novel about the Toronto arrangement was that the student who wished to do additional work in certain subjects was excused from doing the regular work in certain others. The innovation came under attack from the representatives of other Ontario universities when the affairs of the University of Toronto were being investigated by a Select Committee of the Legislature in 1860. Daniel Wilson, Toronto's professor of history and English literature, explained to the committee why the step had been taken:

... the one aim of the Senate, and of the College Council, has been to devise a system of study whereby the youth of this Province may acquire those higher branches of education best calculated to fit them for becoming intelligent and useful members of the community. In Canada, at least, education must be practical. It may be all very well for certain Oxford men, and their indiscriminating admirers, to maintain that the highest aim of a perfect collegiate training consists in the mastery of classical learning, but the scholarship of Oxford, if forced without restriction or choice on the youth of Canada, would in most cases prove of comparatively little practical avail. Nevertheless, let me not be misunderstood. I have freely admitted that the standard of matriculation, or the entrance examination, has been lowered; but I have not admitted, and I do most positively deny, that *the standard of education* has been lowered. A student who goes through the whole classical course of the University will compare favourably with a graduate of equal ability in any other University in the British empire; and if, in the exercise of options, he abandons classics at the prescribed point in his course, he can only do so in order to take in lieu of classics the defined substitutes of modern languages, natural sciences, and mathematics, which will no less thoroughly train his mind, and in many cases will supply him with far more useful acquirements for the future course he is to pursue. The English Universities, under their old rigid system, turned out a class of educated men, with whom too frequently the people found little sympathy; but the Scottish University system, by the very laxness which left the student's choice of studies so much to himself as practically to amount to a comprehensive system of options, has made *an educated people*; and the latter I conceive is what Canada desires.[13]

Despite a month of hearings, this parliamentary committee reached no decision about anything. Wilson and his colleagues were left free to continue with their experiment.

By 1877 they were able to announce in the Calendar that "there are two ordinary modes of proceeding to the degree of BA, viz: (1) by taking a Pass Course; or (2) by taking an Honour Course." There were five honours courses (or departments as they were then called): classics, mathematics, modern languages with history, natural sciences, and mental and moral philosophy with civil polity. Whichever of the two modes the student selected in proceeding to his degree, his course was largely prescribed. He was required to take so many years of pass English, so many years of honours English, so many years of French or German, so many years of French and German, and so on. The element of choice was in the selection of the course, not within the course itself. A higher standard was also expected of the student taking an honours course; a student who failed in honours could be transferred to the pass course.

As the years went by, additional honours departments or courses were authorized: oriental languages in 1888, political science in 1891, history and also English and history in 1895. By 1904 there were fourteen, by 1939 thirty-one, by 1965 thirty-seven. In 1965–6 just over half the students in the Faculty of Arts and Science were enrolled in an honours course.

As will be explained in the section on teacher training,[14] the development of honours courses received a strong stimulus in the 1890s with the decision of the Department of Education to base the academic qualifications for the secondary school specialist teaching certificate on the possession of an honours degree, and since this decision has never been changed the stimulus has continued for over seventy years. In particular, this influenced the universities other than Toronto to offer honours courses as well as the pass, general, or fixed course to which some of them were, and perhaps still are, primarily devoted. The position of Queen's in the late nineteenth century is a case in point:

One of the points at issue between Toronto and the outlying universities was the comparative merits of the special and the fixed courses. Speaking broadly, University College laid stress on honour work, and to give students opportunity to pursue certain lines with some thoroughness, permitted them to omit certain other studies, or at least to be content with a slighter acquaintance with them. The outlying colleges prescribed a fixed or balanced course, which all were obliged to take. It provided an excellent general education, but nowhere gave specialized instruction, while the University College honour courses took students a respectable length into the department of their choice, at the risk, as the outlying colleges invariably pointed out, of leaving them ill-informed on other essential subjects. The honour course met with the approval of the provincial education department, as well as of the general public, and the absence of honours in the degrees of the outlying institutions was one reason for the preponderance of Toronto men in the high schools. Grant now moved towards the honour course by instituting a system of options which at first enabled students to lean towards the side of the curriculum which their tastes caused them to prefer. The tendency continued as the staff was increased, until at length Queen's carried the principle of specialization to considerable lengths.[15]

An honours programme was offered at Queen's in five departments in 1879 but it was not until the 1890s that the courses became clearly defined. Victoria, which had permitted additional work for honours since 1861, announced honours courses in classics, moderns, orientals, mathematics, and English and history in 1884. In the same year Trinity increased by three the subjects available for the BA with honours, which had been offered since 1854. In 1885 Ottawa introduced a BA with honours in five areas. McMaster, on opening in 1890, made provision for honours for students who were able "without undue effort" to reach and maintain a standard of 75 per cent in the regular course. Honours courses were available at Western when its Faculty of Arts, which had had a brief existence in the 1880s, was reopened in 1895. Without exception, universities which have been opened since 1939 have made provision for honours courses.

In the 1860s and 1870s the honours courses at Toronto required the same number of years to complete as the general or pass course but by 1890 they involved an extra year. This pattern was followed by the other universities as they developed their honours courses. The apparent consequence has been the addition of a year of study for graduate degrees since the universities, again led by Toronto, which was the first university in the province to develop a large school of graduate studies, have tended to demand the honours BA for admission to the one-year MA or MSc programmes and to require of applicants with a general BA or BSc a special make-up year. Since admission to the doctoral programmes is based on possession of a master's degree, it too, apparently, has been lengthened. However, an examination of the age of students receiving the honours BA reveals that a very large number are twenty-one, indicating sixteen years of schooling from entry to Grade 1 at age six. The explanation lies in the fact that about 20 per cent of the pupils entering Grade 1 complete the thirteen grades in twelve years having accelerated at some stage along the way. The accelerators are, of course, the intellectually gifted group and the ones who are most likely to proceed to university.

TEACHER TRAINING

The Development of Normal Schools

It was not necessary in 1867 to take any formal instruction in order to be certified as a teacher. The only course offered was that provided at the Normal School at Toronto, which lasted for five months and which was offered twice each year. But more than half of the over 5,000 candidates who had been admitted to the Normal School since its establishment in 1847 had already had practical experience as teachers and were the possessors of the County Board Certificate. A proportion of them presumably had "attended" one of the township model schools: these were simply elementary schools which, by authority of the Common School Act of 1850, a municipal council could designate as schools where teachers or potential teachers could observe what was going on.

The objectives of the Normal School which was located at Toronto and of the two model schools (one for boys, one for girls) appended to it for purposes of observation and practice teaching had been clearly stated by the Chief Superintendent:

The Normal and Model Schools were not designed to educate young persons, but to *train teachers*, both theoretically and practically, for conducting schools throughout the Province, in cities and towns as well as townships. They are not constituted, as are most of the Normal Schools in both Europe and North America, to impart the preliminary education requisite for teaching. That preparatory education is supposed to have been attained in the ordinary public or private schools. The entrance examination to the Normal School requires this.[16]

That the entrance requirement was taken seriously can be deduced from the fact that twenty-four applicants were rejected for the two sessions of 1867 (277 were admitted). On the other hand, we have noted earlier that secondary education in Ontario was not established on a firm basis until the passing of the 1871 Act. At his most sanguine, Ryerson would not have argued that the course of study offered in the common schools of Ontario in 1867 contributed "the preliminary education requisite for teaching."

What is of particular significance here, however, is the heavy emphasis upon *professional* training. "The object . . . is . . . to do for the teacher what apprenticeship does for the mechanic, the artist, the physician, the lawyer—to teach him, theoretically and practically, how to do the work of his profession." This view has characterized the approach to teacher training adopted by the authorities in Ontario from 1847 to the present day.

Ryerson had endeavoured to provide comparable training for secondary school teachers but his efforts had been unsuccessful. The Model Grammar School which was opened in 1858 was closed for want of students in 1863. The first of two attempts (there was a second in 1880) to convert Upper Canada College, a private school whose endowment derived from public funds, into a model school aborted in 1860. The majority of grammar school headmasters and assistants in 1867 had a university degree, and a number of others had the Normal School certificate. It must be remembered, of course, that until 1871 the grammar schools were only vaguely under public supervision.

In 1872 Ryerson proposed three additional normal schools, at London, Kingston, and Ottawa. Had this proposal been adopted, it is possible that normal school training would have been required of all elementary school teachers. But only one normal school was added, at Ottawa, and instead, county model schools were introduced in 1877. The county model school, of which there were forty-seven by 1880, developed from the old township model school and was an elementary school where observation and practice teaching could be carried out under the supervision of the principal and his staff. The model school "course," which ran for fourteen weeks from September to December, led to the Third Class Certificate which was granted by the county. Initially, the time the principal could devote each day to his students-in-training was limited to the period before

9:00 a.m. and after 4:00 p.m. since he continued to carry full responsibility for his duties as principal, including a full teaching load. But, in 1885, he was freed for a half day during the model school term, and by 1907 when it was decided to close the county model schools he was normally devoting his whole attention during the fourteen weeks to the students-in-training.

Reviewing the development of teacher training in Ontario in 1941, J. M. McCutcheon argued that the establishment of county model schools was a practical necessity which produced practical results:

For thirty years, the County Model Schools performed a useful service in the interests of elementary education. During that time they prepared more than thirty-six thousand teachers for the elementary schools. Their popularity was due in no small measure to the fact that they were easily accessible and relatively inexpensive. They introduced the idea of compulsory training for teachers. When these schools were inaugurated in 1877, only seventeen per cent of the teachers in the province then employed in the public schools had any professional training whatsoever. At that time it would have been impractical to have required normal school training for every teacher. The essential requirement was that all teachers should be provided with some professional training, and this the County Model Schools were able to supply.[17]

Practical necessity often does lead to practical results, but how practical is practical? The establishment of the county model schools insured that there would be teachers for the schools of the province, but whether they were good teachers or not is a different question. Certainly many of them were birds of passage. The Third Class Certificate was only valid for three years and to obtain a permanent certificate, either First or Second Class, it was necessary to attend a normal school. Since the average annual attendance at the county model schools during the thirty years of their existence was twelve hundred, while the average attendance at the normal schools during this same period was three hundred, it can be seen that the dropout rate from the "profession" was extraordinarily high. W. J. Karr, an earlier historian of teacher training in Ontario, had this comment to make in 1916:

Here was an example of great educational waste. The training schools were devoting their energies to training teachers, three-quarters of whom gave only three years or less of service in return for that training. The frequent change of teachers in the schools, with the resulting loss of time in making new adjustments, still further increased this educational waste. It was apparent that this waste could be prevented only by requiring a longer period of training, granting a permanent certificate upon its completion, and thus encouraging a longer period of service in the profession.[18]

In 1908 Ryerson's proposal of 1872 was finally adopted. Three normal schools were opened that year (Hamilton, Peterborough, Stratford) and a fourth at North Bay in 1909 bringing the total to seven, since a normal school at London had been opened in 1900. The county model schools had now been abolished, but a few provincial model schools, under the direct control of the Department of Education, had been established for the benefit of rural school sections which were unable to pay salaries sufficient to attract normal school graduates. The graduates of these provincial model schools, which were discontinued in 1924, received a Limited Third Class Certificate, valid for five years. In 1907 the department had also authorized the first of several English-French model schools, whose graduates received a Third Class Certificate valid for three years in schools in which French as well as English was an official language of instruction. But the great majority of teachers now attended one of the normal schools where they took a course which since 1904 had been lengthened to a full academic year and which normally led to an interim Second

Class Certificate that became permanent after two years of teaching deemed "successful" by the inspector.

From 1875 to 1890 the normal schools offered a second course of five months, for which the Second Class Certificate was prerequisite, leading to the First Class Certificate, but in 1890 this work was taken over by the newly established School of Pedagogy. The First Class Certificate course was again offered in the normal schools from 1920 to 1936. In the latter year the Second Class Certificate course was discontinued in all but one of the normal schools and a single course was henceforth offered leading to the Elementary School Teacher's Certificate. The exception was the University of Ottawa Normal School, which had been opened in 1928 to serve the needs, hitherto somewhat gropingly provided for by the English-French model schools, of schools where French was a language of instruction. The Second Class Certificate has been retained for the graduates of the one-year course, for students admitted from Grade 12 by the University of Ottawa and, since its establishment in 1963 to share in this work, by the Sudbury Teachers' College.

Let us return again to the decision of 1877 which "for practical reasons" postponed for thirty years the concentration of elementary school teacher training in the normal schools. What were the consequences, both practical and theoretical, of this decision? One certainly was the division of members of the profession into first, second, and third class citizens. A second was the encouragement of the emphasis upon professional training. Had the normal schools been required in the last quarter of the nineteenth century to provide a course for the majority rather than the minority of potential teachers, it is entirely possible that the resulting course would have included a substantial amount of academic content since many of the potential teachers would have been recognized as deficient in that "preliminary education requisite for teaching" to which Ryerson referred in his 1867 report. What in fact happened was that the normal school programme of 1867 had forty more years to develop its methodological emphasis, and when in 1908 the normal schools were faced with the necessity of providing for the preparation of all elementary school teachers, the mould was set.

Has there been any fundamental change in the essential emphasis of the basic course offered to elementary school teachers in Ontario in the past one hundred years? Karr's description[19] of the course in 1916 indicates no change in the first half century and the comment of McCutcheon in 1941 brings us within twenty-five years of the present:

The whole Normal School programme, including instruction in teaching technique, academic reviews, practice-teaching, and opportunities for observation, is now so organized as to contribute in the most economical and effective manner to the technical and professional equipment of the teachers-in-training.[20]

The report submitted in 1966 by the Committee, which the Minister of Education appointed in 1964 to study elementary teacher training in Ontario, indicates that the change of name from Normal School to Teachers' College in 1953 was not accompanied by any substantial change in emphasis:

From the earliest years of the public educational system in Ontario, those charged with the responsibility for teacher education have had the task of resolving the problems of recruitment and supply of teachers. In the early stage of our free school system the teacher, although not infrequently a man of culture and good will, was sometimes ill-trained or ill-suited to the life of the community. In fact, formal education was often looked upon as a matter of little significance and importance, and the teacher was regarded and paid accordingly.

From such a beginning the profession has made considerable progress, but it has not yet been able to shake itself entirely free from this unhappy legacy. Neither the true importance of the teacher's role in society nor the scholarship and training necessary to prepare him for that role has been adequately recognized. The elementary school teacher has been seen by some people as a dispenser of facts and a drillmaster of the three R's. Anyone who could maintain reasonable order, who had a way with younger children, and who knew a bit more than the basic elementary school curriculum was considered by such people as a fair prospect for teaching.

During the last quarter century there has been not only an unprecedented growth in the body of knowledge but also a tremendous increase in school population. The need for every child to have an opportunity for education has demanded a programme of expansion in which the necessity for providing physical accommodation has taken precedence over the updating of the curriculum and the improvement of the preparation of teachers.

Whereas most of the other countries in the western world have for some time been aiming, with varying success, at goals in teacher education of two, three, or four years beyond high school, Ontario has so far continued to prepare its teachers in a one-year program following secondary school graduation. It is not surprising, therefore, that elementary school teachers in Ontario have not won the professional status achieved by teachers in some other jurisdictions.[21]

The Separation of Elementary and Secondary Teacher Training

It is possible, too, that an expansion of the normal schools in the 1870s would have led to the linking of elementary and secondary school teacher training in Ontario and to the avoidance of the complete isolation of the normal schools from the universities. Certainly the times were propitious for joint action in the field of education. It was in the late 70s and early 80s that there developed for the first time an interest in the study of education as an academic subject. G. Compayré at the Sorbonne, S. S. Laurie at Edinburgh, R. H. Quick at Cambridge, G. Stanley Hall at Harvard, and Johns Hopkins were the pioneers in the field. Education was one of the subjects proposed for the BA in the University of Toronto Federation Act of 1887.

It was also in the 80s that provision was made in Ontario for the training of secondary school teachers. An act of 1885 authorized the establishment of training institutes, somewhat on the model of the county model schools. Potential high school teachers could attend certain collegiate institutes during the fall term where they would receive instruction in the teaching of high school subjects and be given opportunities to observe the work of experienced teachers and under supervision to do some teaching themselves. The combination of few applicants, lack of professional training for this type of work on the part of the instructors (the principal and staff of the collegiate), and inevitable interference with the regular programme of the collegiate resulted in the discontinuance of the training institutes in 1890 and the establishment of a School of Pedagogy in their place. This school was located in the Toronto Normal School; it failed to develop properly, partly because the facilities for practice-teaching were inadequate and partly because the progamme remained a voluntary one. Both of these limitations were removed when in 1895 certification of high school teachers became obligatory and when in 1897 the school was transferred, as the Ontario Normal College, to Hamilton where it was closely associated with the Hamilton Collegiate Institute, whose principal was also its principal and whose department heads were its lecturers. The only problem then was that the instructors were engaged part-time in the work of the Normal College; hence in 1907 the discontinuance of the Ontario Normal College and the establishment of faculties of education, with full-time staffs, at Queen's University and the University of Toronto. Both faculties were financed by the Department of Education. In 1920, the Queen's faculty was discontinued and the Toronto faculty was transformed into the

Ontario College of Education. For the next forty years all secondary school teacher training was concentrated in this college, which continued to be financed by the Department of Education.

There was surely the possibility in the 1890s when the School of Pedagogy was housed in the Toronto Normal School, for teacher training to be viewed in the round and as a continuing process, rather than in segmented and static fashion. Perhaps the chances would have been better if the Normal School's nose had not been pressed quite so closely to its own little grindstone, if it had been responsible for the training of all elementary school teachers rather than just a small proportion of them. In any event, the opportunity was not seized and the two branches of teacher training in Ontario went their separate ways. In due course the secondary school branch developed a connection with the universities. The elementary branch has yet to do so.

The Development of the Specialist Certificate

It will be recalled that what originally distinguished a collegiate institute from a high school and what placed it therefore in a preferred position with respect to the annual grant was the presence at the former of four teachers and a minimum of sixty students pursuing the classics.[22] On January 1st, 1885 the ground rules were changed. Henceforth the following were required:

(1) Suitable school buildings, outbuildings, grounds, and appliances for physical training [the physical education requirement was the novelty here].

(2) A library, containing standard books of reference bearing on the subjects of the programme.

(3) A laboratory, with all necessary chemicals, and apparatus for teaching the subjects of elementary science.

(4) Four masters, at least, each of whom shall be

specially qualified in one of the following departments: Classics, mathematics, natural science and modern languages, including English.

(5) The other members of the teaching staff must possess such qualifications as will secure thorough instruction in all subjects of the curriculum of studies for the time being sanctioned by the Education Department for collegiate institutes.

One of the reasons for establishing the training institutes in 1885 was to provide for the qualification of these "specially qualified Masters"; sixteen of the twenty-one students who attended the first year qualified as specialists, and of the one hundred and eighty-four who attended the training institutes during the five years of their existence more than three-quarters obtained specialist standing; forty-seven in mathematics, twenty-nine in classics, twenty-eight in each of English and modern languages (French and German), and fourteen in science.

Responsibility for the preparation of specialists was assumed by the School of Pedagogy when it replaced the training institutes in 1890. By 1893, a collegiate institute was required to have a specialist in *each* of the four departments and the specialist was required to have both professional and academic qualifications. On the professional side he was required to take a special course in the methods of teaching his high school subject or subjects and a higher standard was required of him than of the non-specialist at the professional examination. The academic qualification was the Senior Leaving Certificate, which was obtained by passing examinations based on a portion of the curriculum of the appropriate departments at the University of Toronto. Thus, for specialist standing the requirements were:

(*a*) English and history—the honour English course of the first and second years, and the pass courses in English and history of the four years, (*b*) mathematics—the pass and honour courses in mathematics and physics of the first and second years,

(*c*) classics—the pass and honour courses in classics of the first and second years,

(*d*) French and German—the pass courses in French and German of the four years, with the honour examination in conversation of the third year, and

(*e*) science—either the honour course in natural science of the first and second years, or the honour course in chemistry and mineralogy of the first and second years with the biology of the first and second years of the natural science course.

English, it will be noted, has been separated from moderns as a specialist subject, and history has been introduced. At first a special examination was set by the Education Department but almost immediately the University of Toronto marks were accepted as fulfilling the requirement. Next, arrangements were made to approve comparable courses at other universities for specialist standing. Then, in 1898, *graduation* from the appropriate honours course at the University of Toronto was required for specialist standing, with equivalent recognition being given to other universities which had courses of equivalent standard.

Possession of an honours degree remains in 1966 the academic qualification for what is now called the High School Assistant's Certificate Type A (Specialist). The requirement of second-class standing in the honours course had been added, and there are now many more specialties than the original five. But the position of 1895 remains essentially unchanged. What have been the consequences?

Since specialist standing has always been rewarded by an increase in salary, and since it has long been an effective requirement for promotion to department head, principal, or inspector, it has been much sought after; in the 1920s as high as seventy per cent of the teachers in the public secondary schools of Ontario were specialists. (The percentage, unfortunately, is much lower today.) The influence of such teachers on secondary education in the province cannot be measured or defined, but it can scarcely be exaggerated. It can also be said that the specialist arrangement has had a very stimulating effect on the enrolment in honours courses at the Ontario universities; had there not been this practical requirement, it is unlikely that the honours course system would have been developed in so many Ontario universities and embraced so many different fields of concentration.

There have also been consequences within the framework of teacher training itself. In Ontario there is no mixing of academic and professional preparation; the professional training of the secondary school teacher comes *after* the student has completed his academic training in a degree course. The requirement of the honours degree for specialist standing has militated against the development of combined arts and education programmes since it is essential to the idea of an honours course that for a given period of time the student's efforts should be concentrated on his academic studies.

The existence of the specialist certificate is also partly responsible for the differences in approach, which have been adopted in the province, to the training of elementary and secondary school teachers. By emphasizing the academic side of the preparation of the secondary school teacher, which is precisely the side which has been underemphasized in the preparation of the elementary school teacher, it has unconsciously widened the gap between them; and by buttressing the four-year honours degree programme it has, again unconsciously, directed attention away from the three-year general degree programme, which is much more within the reach of the elementary school teacher. There is another way in which the same point can be put;

one of the reasons that the universities have devoted so little time to the needs of elementary school teachers is that they have devoted so much to the needs of the teachers in the secondary schools.

The MacLeod Report

It is now apparent that a very different approach to teacher education will be adopted by the province of Ontario in the second century of its existence. In September 1964, the Minister of Education appointed a special committee under the chairmanship of C. R. MacLeod, Superintendent of Public Schools and Assistant Director of Education, Windsor, to examine and report on the preparation of teachers for the elementary schools of Ontario. The specific terms of reference of the MacLeod Committee focussed attention on the programmes being offered in the existing teachers' colleges and made no mention of the preparation of secondary school teachers, but the committee was assured by the Minister "that it should feel free to examine all aspects of elementary school teacher education and in addition to consider the co-ordination and integration of teacher education programmes for elementary and secondary school teachers."[23]

After nearly two years of study the committee submitted its report in March 1966. Its recommendations, if adopted, will transform teacher education in the province. All teacher education would be provided by the universities, a single college or faculty of education would be responsible for the training of both elementary and secondary school teachers, and all elementary school teachers would be required to hold a university degree. The committee recognized that these changes, and particularly the last mentioned, could not be adopted at a single point in time; consequently, it proposed that the full programme be introduced in three stages. In the first, all elementary school teachers would be required to qualify for normal university admission and then complete a two-year course consisting of one year of academic study and one year of professional preparation. In the second phase two years of academic study would be required in addition to the year of professional training, and in the third, three years of academic study, in other words, a general BA or BSc degree.

So far the MacLeod Report has simply been received. But the tenor of the Minister's remarks in the Legislature when reporting its publication indicate that the basic recommendations of the committee will be implemented: "The department and the Minister are in complete agreement with the general programme suggested and it will be the policy of my department to implement plans to this end as quickly as possible."[24] It is felt that the full programme could be in effect by 1975.

VOCATIONAL TRAINING

From 1867 to 1900

In 1867 the only institutions in Ontario exclusively concerned with preparing students for a vocation were the Normal School, the Toronto School of Medicine, the Ontario Veterinary College, and a number of theological colleges or seminaries. The Ontario Veterinary College was a private venture which had been opened at Toronto by Andrew Smith in 1864; so was the Toronto School of Medicine, which was affiliated with the University of Toronto and which would become, in 1887, its Faculty of Medicine. The faculties of medicine and law at Queen's University were also proprietary schools, since the university bore no responsibility for their financing. Two-year courses in agriculture and in engineering had been listed since 1857 in the calendar of University College, at this time the only teaching element of the University of Toronto, but few candidates had presented themselves; in 1867, only one student was examined in agriculture, and only one in engineering. In addition to theological colleges like Knox and seminaries like St. Michael's, there were faculties of theology at Ottawa, Queen's, and Trinity. Some of the many mechanics institutes spread about the province may have been giving instruction in practical matters.

During the final thirty years of the nineteenth century, there was a very considerable expansion in this area. Except in medicine, where by 1900 there were faculties at Queen's, Toronto, and Western Ontario, the involvement of the universities was nominal rather than direct, taking the form of affiliation arrangements which enabled university degrees to be granted to students in independently controlled institutions. By 1900 Toronto's affiliates included two institutions organized and controlled by the Government (the School of Technology, later the School of Practical Science, 1872; the Ontario Agricultural College, 1874), two sponsored by a profession (Royal College of Dental Surgeons, 1875; Ontario College of Pharmacy, 1882), and three conservatories of music (one in Hamilton, two in Toronto), organized in the mid-1880s. The Kingston School of Mines, established in 1893 with financial support from the Government, had been affiliated with Queen's from the outset.

Quite independent of the universities was the growth of training schools for nurses, of which there were twelve by 1900. The first of these was a school established at St. Catharines by Dr. Theophilus Mack in 1874 with a staff of two "Nightingale nurses" brought over from England and a student body of two "probationers." More important, since it established the pattern of *hospital* schools of nursing, was the school opened at the Toronto General Hospital in 1881; by 1890 there were similar schools at Brockville, Chatham, Guelph, Hamilton, London, and Peterborough.

In 1890 a school, which was independent of a hospital, was opened at Ottawa, the Lady Stanley Institute, but it was located adjacent to the Carleton County General Protestant Hospital and in 1901 it was absorbed by it. The other schools established by 1900 were at the Hospital for Sick Children in Toronto, St. Michael's Hospital in Toronto, and St. Joseph's Hospital in Guelph. At the latter two, the school was directed by the Sisters of St. Joseph, a Roman Catholic religious order.

The course provided for the student nurse at the Toronto General Hospital when it opened in 1881 was essentially an apprenticeship. She received some instruction in the wards and attended a lecture twice a week, but mostly she nursed. The "course" lasted two years. In 1896 it was extended to three years, with formal instruction consisting of eighty-four hours of lectures on "practical nursing" and one hundred and nineteen on such subjects as anatomy, physiology, communicable diseases, and obstetrics. The two-year course was the normal one in the Ontario hospital schools of nursing in 1900, and the arrangements were similar to those at the Toronto General.

By 1900 there were also in Ontario five art schools, one of which continues today as the Ontario College of Art. It dates from 1876 when the Ontario Society of Artists opened a school in its own building with the assistance of $1,000 grant from the Government. The grant, which made it possible to operate the school without tuition fees, rose steadily each year ($4,500 in 1880), and in 1882 the Ontario School of Art and Design was transferred to the Normal School building where it was managed jointly by the society and the department. Its activities at this time were described by a visiting Englishman inspecting technical education in North America:

The Ontario School of Art in Toronto is an institution supported by the Legislature of the Province, for the purpose of imparting special instruction, embracing subjects in science and art teaching suitable to mechanics, and bearing on their employment. There are evening classes adapted to working men. This excellent school is the commencement of an institution similar in object and appliances to our South Kensington Museum. Although in its infancy, the instruction given is evidently valued by the various trades of the city. Out of 121 students last year, one half were engaged in trades and manufactures; the remainder studying as teachers. The instruction is confined to drawing in every branch, and designing. I was particularly struck with the manifest relation between the work done in the school and industrial pursuits.[25]

The connection of the Ontario Society of Artists with the school was severed in 1884 and for the next two years it was managed by the Department of Education. In 1886 it was incorporated as the Ontario School of Art, under the terms of an act which authorized grants to art schools which complied with certain regulations of the Department of Education. By this time, too, an elaborate system of departmental examinations, leading to certificates in primary, advanced, and industrial art courses and in mechanical drawing, had been worked out and could be written by students in public and private secondary schools as well as in schools of art. In 1900, 289 students were registered for the primary course in five schools of art, 283 in the advanced course, 108 in mechanical drawing, and 122 in industrial art.

One other institution remains to be mentioned: the law school established by the Upper Canada Law Society at its headquarters, Osgoode Hall, in 1889. Students wishing to qualify for admission to the bar, which was, and is, controlled by the society, were required to attend the school for a period of time.

There appeared in 1893 a statement by the Deputy Minister of Education which outlined the policy of the Government with respect to vocational training. It is worth quoting at length since the policy remained in effect until fairly recent times:

The design of the Government of Ontario has been to provide a general education for all classes, and such a training as will enable any student who so desires to take a professional course. With the exception of the fees required, the Academic training is provided at the public expense, but it is not the policy of the Province to provide free for students a professional education. Perhaps the only exceptions to this principle are to be found in the case of the Agricultural College and the School of Practical Science. As the interests of the farmers are largely bound up with those of the Province generally, the subject of Agriculture has due recognition in the Public School curriculum, and liberal grants from the Legislature have been made to Farmers' Institutes. The expenditure annually made in behalf of the Agricultural College at Guelph is justified by the growing importance of a knowledge of Scientific Agriculture to the farming community, and by the high position gained by that Institution among Colleges with a similar object. Encouragement is also generously given in the Public and High Schools, as well as in the Mechanics' Institutes, to drawing as a preliminary training for various industrial pursuits, and the erection and equipment of the School of Practical Science have been demanded in view of the immense mineral resources of the Province, which are now only beginning to be fully valued.

In the case of other professions, such as law, medicine, dentistry, etc., the intention has been to require those who take up those pursuits to gain, at their own expense, the knowledge or training necessary. These professions have, however, been placed by law on such a basis as to guarantee to the public that those who follow such callings shall be persons of good education and high professional acquirements. The statutes give largely to the members of each profession the power to make regulations regarding the examinations to be passed by those desiring to enter such profession.[26]

From 1900 to 1939

Between 1900 and 1939 the main developments in the vocational field took place either at the universities or, as has been noted earlier,[27] within the context of the secondary school. The Ontario College of Art emerged as the single centre for the study of art and the hospital schools of nursing proliferated.

At the universities there was sound development of medicine at Queen's, Toronto, and Western; of engineering at Queen's and Toronto; of agriculture and veterinary medicine at the Ontario Agricultural College; of business at Western; of household science at Toronto and the Ontario Agricultural College; and of architecture (within engineering), dentistry, forestry, social work, and music at Toronto. Towards the end of the period, library science and nursing were introduced at Toronto. Ottawa and McMaster confined their activity to arts and theology.

In 1900 the training of nurses was a venture carried on by a dozen hospitals essentially for their own benefit; the effort guaranteed the presence of the junior staff required to carry on the work of the hospital. The Government was not involved, and neither was the nursing profession. This latter is not surprising, since in 1900 there was no nursing profession in any organized sense.

A Graduate Nurses Association began to be formed in 1904, it was incorporated in 1908, and in 1925 became the Registered Nurses Association of Ontario. Its early efforts were devoted to persuading the Government that there should be official registration of all nurses. In 1914 the term "registered nurse" was authorized to be used by graduates of approved hospital schools of nursing and only by such graduates, but it was not until 1922 that registration became mandatory and dependent upon the achievement of specified minimum standards. The 1922 Act Respecting the Registration of Nurses in Ontario placed control with the Department of Health, which was established by the Government in 1923. It was not until 1951 that the nurses, through their Association, became responsible for entry to the profession. They did, however, play an increasingly important role in defining the curriculum and the regulations of the hospital schools through official representation on the Council of Nursing Education which the Department of Health established to advise it on such matters.

The number of hospital schools of nursing increased greatly during the first three decades of the new century; there were eighty-nine in Ontario in 1932 when G. M. Weir's *Survey of Nursing Education in Canada* was published. Weir found that twenty-seven of these were in hospitals with less than fifty beds and that, despite a regulation requiring a staff of at least three registered nurses, eleven Ontario schools had staffs of either one or two. One of Weir's major recommendations was that no hospital be authorized to conduct a training school unless it had at least seventy-five beds and unless its staff included five (and preferably six) registered nurses. Action on the recommendations rested, of course, with each province. There was action in Ontario; by 1939 the number of hospital schools had been reduced to approximately sixty, each of which provided a three-year course, with entry from junior matriculation. The course of study approximated the four hundred and ninety-five hours of classroom instruction which Weir had recommended, the great bulk of these being concentrated in the first year and particularly in a "probationary period" of four to six months when the student spent most of her time in the classroom or under direct supervision.

The Ontario College of Art assumed its present name in 1912. By this time the other art schools which had sprung up in the 1880s had disappeared, their activities being absorbed within the developing programmes of the secondary schools. Early in the century, the course of study was extended to four years. By 1939 full-time enrolment had reached one hundred and forty and options were available in drawing and painting, sculpture, commercial art, and interior decoration. The majority of students entered with junior matriculation.

From 1939 to 1965

Since 1939 vocational education has been greatly developed and expanded in all the institutions so far mentioned. There are still approximately the same number of hospital schools of nursing but the enrolment has risen from 3,998 in 1939 to 8,774 in 1965. The Ontario College of Art has found it necessary to establish a maximum enrolment of one thousand and its diploma programmes now number six: advertising art, painting, industrial design, interior design and decoration, material arts, and sculpture. In the universities there are now four schools of medicine (with a fifth to be opened at McMaster in 1967), eight schools of engineering, four schools of law (in addition to Osgoode Hall), six schools of nursing, six of physical and health education (with a seventh opened at Guelph in September, 1966), two of library science (with a third to open at Western in 1968), eight of commerce and business administration, four of household science, two of social work (with a third opened at Windsor in September 1966), and two of journalism. A second dental school will be opened at Western in 1967. Agriculture and veterinary medicine remain concentrated at Guelph, while Toronto continues to provide the only courses in architecture, forestry, and pharmacy. There has also been a striking development of vocational programmes in the secondary schools. But the most significant fact of the past quarter century in the realm of vocational training in Ontario has been the creation of new institutions specifically designed to provide technological training; first, institutes of technology, then institutes of trades, then vocational centres, and finally colleges of applied arts and technology.

The first of these institutions was the Provincial Institute of Mining, organized at Haileybury in 1944. Actually the new institution replaced a programme which had been conducted in Haileybury High School for nearly twenty years. Two years later a Provincial Institute of Textiles was established at Hamilton. In 1948, the Lakehead Technical Institute at Port Arthur, and the Ryerson Institute of Technology at Toronto were opened, the latter being based on the Training and Re-establishment Institute set up by the federal government for returning veterans at the end of the Second World War.

In the same year the Minister declared that "the provision of technical education between the levels provided in the vocational schools and in the universities is now an accepted responsibility of the Department of Education."[28] Since 1948, the Institute of Textiles has been renamed the Hamilton Institute of Technology (1956), and additional institutes have been opened at Ottawa (1957), Windsor (1958), and Kirkland Lake (1962).

All these institutes offer three-year courses to students with Grade 12 standing. With the exception of Haileybury, which from the beginning largely confined its activities to mining, and the Lakehead Institute, which has emphasized forest technology, all the institutes have been offering courses in engineering technology and in business administration. Hamilton, in addition, has provided courses in textile technology and industrial management. Only Ryerson has offered a *wide* range of courses; engineering (in half a dozen branches), business administration, journalism, television arts, nursing, laboratory technician, home economics, and several more. And only Ryerson has developed into a large and booming institution. Its full-time enrolment in 1965–6 was 3,687 contrasted with 2,536 in the other five combined. Its part-time enrolment (evening classes) was almost four times larger than that of its rivals—7,540 to 2,146. The demand for entrance to Ryerson has been so heavy that arrangements have been made with several Toronto secondary schools to provide the first year of its engineering course. The very real difference between Ryerson and the other institutes is reflected in the recent decision to give it a new name and a new status as a polytechnic institute with its own Board of Governors.

A change in the arrangement for apprenticeship training led to the establishment of the Provincial Institute of Trades at Toronto in 1951. It will be recalled that the Apprenticeship Act of 1928 assigned responsibility for the academic portion of the apprentice's programme to the (secondary) vocational schools but after the war this work was largely concentrated, first, in the Training and Re-establishment Institute established at Toronto in 1945 as a rehabilitation centre for veterans, and from 1948 on at the Ryerson Institute, into which the rehabilitation centre evolved. Ryerson's rapidly increasing enrolment and rapidly expanding curriculum made the transfer of this work to a separate institution necessary, and the new Institute of Trades was the result. Steady increase in its enrolment led to its effective subdivision into three parts in 1962—the Provincial Institute of Trades, the Provincial Institute of Automotive and Allied Trades, and the Provincial Institute of Trades and Occupations. All these were located in Toronto, but additional institutes of trades at Ottawa and London were planned. By the time these opened (September 1964) it had been decided to call them "Ontario Vocational Centres":

The name "Ontario Vocational Centre" was selected for these new technical institutes to provide a better indication of the scope of the vocational courses they offer. Along with the Provincial Institute of Trades, the Provincial Institute of Automotive and Allied Trades, and the Provincial Institute of Trades and Occupations, all located in Toronto, the new Ontario Vocational Centres offer courses in four main divisions: technical courses for apprentices in the certified trades, as designated by the Department of Labour of Ontario; pre-employment courses in non-certified trades and trades approved for vocational training under the Dominion-Provincial Technical and Vocational Training Agreement; two-year engineering-technical courses for secondary-school graduates; and post-secondary business and commercial courses.[29]

A third vocational centre was opened at Sault Ste. Marie in 1965, and a fourth was planned to be opened at Hamilton in 1966. The Hamilton Vocational Centre, it was decided, would be located on the same campus as the Hamilton Institute of Technology though the two institutions would be separately administered. But by the time September 1966 came along, the Department of Education had announced its intention of establishing a network of colleges of applied arts and technology throughout the province and the two Hamilton institutions have been embraced within the Hamilton College of Applied Arts and Technology.

The Colleges of Applied Arts and Technology

In 1962 the enrolment in the institutes of technology was a little under four thousand and the plan of the Department of Education was to increase the accommodation to six thousand in the course of the next four or five years. The need for a much more rapid expansion of the facilities for technological training was argued in a report prepared by the presidents of the universities of Ontario in 1962 and published in March 1963.[30] This report was primarily concerned with outlining a plan whereby the province could be assured that there would be a sufficient number of places for the greatly increased number of high school matriculants which, in the light of the rising birth rate and the heavy immigration of the post-war years, could be expected from 1965 on. The presidents stated that sufficient places would be available for each year through to 1970 if (*a*) the

existing universities were expanded in specific ways, (b)
two new universities were established (Brock and Trent),
and (c) the University of Toronto established new liberal
arts and science colleges on the eastern and western out-
skirts of Toronto (Scarborough and Erindale). But the
report also called attention to the importance of other forms
of post-secondary education, notably the teachers' colleges,
the hospital schools of nursing, and the institutes of technology, and a strong plea was made for a full-scale study of
technological education in the province. "We think that the
relations of vocational secondary schools and technological
institutes—indeed, the entire development of technological
and technical education in Ontario—should be investigated
in depth, by a competent and representative group, backed
by a fact-finding and research staff. Direction, co-ordination
and research are sorely needed in this field."[31]

The publication of this report initiated a public debate
on the community college question which continued for
the next two years. It was argued on one side that the proper
way to provide both for the additional university places
required and for the expansion of technological training
was to develop community colleges which would make
available to high school graduates both the first two years of
a university course and two- or three-year technological
courses. But it was also argued that combining the two
types of programme in a single institution would be detri-
mental to both, that the undergraduate programme offered
would be inferior to that provided by a university (since
library and laboratory resources would be inadequate to
attract well-qualified staff), and that the technological
programme would suffer because first priority would be
given to the demands of the university programme with its
supposedly higher prestige value. As I say, this debate
went on for two years; it could be said that it is still going
on. A decision against the community college concept and

in favour of a separation of university and technological
work was apparently taken in March 1965 with the Minister
of Education's announcement that a network of colleges of
applied arts and technology would be established throughout the province. These colleges would concentrate upon
technological and technical education, and undergraduate
instruction would remain the responsibility of universities.
Arrangements would, however, be made whereby graduates
of the new colleges would be eligible, under certain conditions, to transfer to universities with advanced standing.
Furthermore, a college of applied arts and technology,
by entering into an affiliation agreement with a university,
could make university courses available to students on its
campus.

It is no easy task to develop a network of post-secondary
institutions designed to provide for the needs in the technological area of a population of seven million, and it is not
surprising that, eighteen months after the announcement,
the picture is not entirely clear. But a good deal has been
done, particularly since March 1966. A Council of Regents
to assist the minister in the planning, establishment, and
co-ordination of the whole programme has been appointed,
the whole province has been divided into nineteen college
regions, it has been decided that the existing institutes of
technology and vocational centres will form the nuclei of
colleges of applied arts and technology in the region in
which they are now located, and two new colleges have
been established, Centennial College of Applied Arts and
Technology, Scarborough, which will open in October 1966,
and Lambton College of Applied Arts and Technology,
Sarnia, which is expected to open in 1967. The situation
in the fall of 1966 is summarized in Table 3.

It will be noted that boards of regents have at the time
of writing been appointed for only eight areas. It is expected
that the remaining boards will be appointed by January 1,

TABLE 3
CAAT Areas in Ontario

Area	Location	Status
1	Counties of Renfrew, Lanark, Carleton, Russell, Prescott	Board of Regents for Algonquin College appointed. Eastern Ontario Institute of Technology and Ontario Vocational Centre, Ottawa, in operation
2	Counties of Frontenac, Leeds, Grenville, Dundas, Stormont, Glengarry	
3	Counties of Lennox and Addington, Hastings, Prince Edward, Northumberland, Peterborough, Haliburton, Victoria	
4	Counties of Ontario and Durham	
5	Townships of Scarborough and East York	Board for Centennial College, Scarborough, appointed. College opened October 1966
6	Townships of Etobicoke and York	
7	Township of North York and municipalities of County of York not forming part of Metropolitan Toronto	Board appointed
8	Counties of Halton and Peel	
9	Counties of Wentworth and Brant and parts of Lincoln and Haldimand	Board appointed. Hamilton Institute of Technology in operation
10	County of Welland and remaining parts of Lincoln and Haldimand	

TABLE 3—concluded

Area	Location	Status
11	Counties of Elgin, Middlesex, Norfolk, Oxford	Board appointed. Ontario Vocational Centre, London in operation
12	Counties of Essex and Kent	Board appointed for St. Clair College. Western Ontario Institute of Technology, Windsor in operation.
13	County of Lambton	Board appointed for Lambton College. College will open in 1967
14 15	Counties of Huron, Perth, Waterloo, Wellington Counties of Bruce, Grey, Dufferin, Simcoe, Districts of Muskoka and Parry Sound	
16	Districts of Algoma, Manitoulin, Sudbury, Nipissing	Board appointed. Ontario Vocational Centre, Sault Ste. Marie, in operation
17	Districts of Cochrane and Timiskaming	Northern Ontario Institute of Technology, Kirkland Lake, and Haileybury School of Mines in operation
18	Districts of Kenora, Rainy River, Thunder Bay	Technical Division of Lakehead University in operation
19	City of Toronto	Ryerson Polytechnic Institute, 3 provincial institutes of trade, and Toronto Board of Education's Adult Education Centre in operation

1967. The responsibility for establishing college locations in each area rests with the Area Board of Governors, subject to the approval of the Council of Regents.

ADULT EDUCATION

There is nothing particularly distinctive about the way in which adult education is presently organized in Ontario and consequently little to be noted in the past which illuminates the present. The chief point to be made is that, though the Department of Education has for over a century interpreted its terms of reference as extending beyond the limits of elementary and secondary schooling, its efforts to provide for the educational needs of adults have been incidental and oblique rather than conscious and clear-cut. There has been consistent evidence of concern but also a consistent tendency to regard adult education as a matter of secondary importance and one which deserves support but not direction. In all fairness it must be said that Ontario's attitude in this regard has been the usual one. How many Canadian provinces, or American states, or European countries have a long record of firm policy with respect to the education of adults? And of those that do, how many have extended the policy to fields other than those reflecting the needs of the farmer?

The most obvious involvement of the Ontario Department of Education in adult education has been in the area of public libraries. As we have earlier noted, the department in 1867 was providing books for free public libraries and mechanics institutes. An Act of 1880 placed the mechanics institutes under the jurisdiction of the department, one of 1882 authorized municipalities to levy a property tax for the support of free public libraries, and one of 1895 converted the mechanics institutes into either

free public libraries (under municipal control), or association libraries (under private control and with a more than
nominal membership fee), and provided for annual grants
to both types of library by the Department of Education.
This policy has been continued ever since. It has had the
effect of encouraging the establishment of libraries in almost
every community in the province, and in the closing decades
of the nineteenth century and the early decades of the
twentieth this was a good thing. But it has also had the
effect of encouraging the continuance of many of them
long after they were capable of providing a proper service
to their community. Many of the small libraries of Ontario
have hopelessly outmoded book stocks, they are open for
only a few hours each week, and the "librarian" has no
professional training. For years the librarians of the province have been arguing at the annual meetings of the
Ontario Library Association and in the pages of the *Ontario
Library Review* that the solution to this problem is to
organize regional libraries with a proper stock of books
and a staff of trained librarians who can provide adequate
service to the small communities of the region from this
central base. Regional library co-operatives were authorized
by an amendment to the Public Libraries Act in 1957 but
it was not until 1963 that any were established in the
southern part of the province and only in 1966 that all
parts of the province were embraced within what is now
called a "regional library system." There are now fourteen
regions (see Table 4).

Each regional library system is to be under the management, regulation, and control of a nine-member board
representing the county library boards of the region and
also the public library boards of the municipalities with
populations of over fifteen thousand, and it is the duty of
this board to improve the standards of library service by
providing a plan for developing and co-ordinating library

TABLE 4
Ontario Library Regions

Region	Location	Status
Eastern Ontario	Carleton, Lanark, Prescott, Renfrew, Russell, Leeds, Grenville, Stormont, Dundas, Glengarry	Established February 1965
Lake Ontario	Frontenac, Haliburton, Hastings, Lennox and Addington, Northumberland, Durham, Peterborough, Prince Edward, Victoria	Established January 1964
Central Ontario	Peel, Ontario, York, exclusive of Metropolitan Toronto	Established July 1965
Metropolitan Toronto	Metropolitan Toronto	In process of being established
South Central	Wentworth, Brant, Halton	Established May 1965
Niagara	Welland, Lincoln, Haldimand	Established July 1963
Lake Erie	Middlesex, Elgin, Norfolk, Oxford	Established December 1963
Southwestern	Essex, Kent, Lambton	Established May 1963
Mid-western	Huron, Perth, Wellington, Waterloo	Established April 1964
Georgian Bay	Bruce, Grey, Dufferin, Simcoe	Established April, 1966
Algonquin	Muskoka, Parry Sound, Nipissing	Established January 1962 (Nipissing included 1964)
North Central	Sudbury, Manitoulin, Algoma	Established May 1960 (Algoma included 1964)
Northeastern	Cochrane, Temiskaming	Established January 1959
Northwestern	Kenora, Rainy River, Thunder Bay	Established June 1956 (Kenora included 1958)

service within the region. As of January 1, 1967 all the association public libraries of the province will be abolished and their assets (and liabilities) turned over to the board of the regional library system which has jurisdiction in the area in which the association library has been located. There were one hundred and fifty-four of these association libraries in 1965 with an average book stock of less than twenty-five hundred volumes.

In 1964 the Ontario Library Association was supplied with funds by the Department of Education to make a thorough study of the whole library system of the province and to make recommendations to the Minister. The association commissioned Francis R. St. John Library Consultants, Inc., a New York firm, to undertake the study, and its report, *Ontario Libraries: a Province-wide Survey and Plan*, was published in March 1966. Among the sixty-three recommendations are three (5, 6, and 7) which propose the absorption of the association libraries within a regional system. There are other recommendations of the St. John Report which have also been implemented in the Public Libraries Act approved in June 1966. The most important are the appointment of a Director of Provincial Library Service and the establishment of an Ontario Provincial Library Council, consisting of nine persons appointed by the Minister of Education and one representative of each of the regional library systems. There are other recommendations of the report which have aroused a good deal of opposition, for example, the proposal that the University of Toronto do all the cataloguing for all the university libraries of the province, and it is unlikely that the entire plan outlined will be adopted. But clearly Ontario will henceforth have a provincial system of library service and the day of public support for the inadequate library is passed.

The mechanics institutes from which the Ontario public

libraries have evolved were intended to be teaching institutions; they did have libraries but the chief objective was
to provide instruction for "mechanics and artisans." When
they were transformed into public libraries the teaching
function was dropped or rather, since classes had never
been either numerous or successful, the pretense that they
were fulfilling a positive role as educational institutions was
abandoned. Since 1895 the public libraries have concentrated upon providing service; they have very willingly made
their physical facilities available to local groups conducting
adult education classes but they have rarely conducted
classes themselves.

Since the 1890s adult education has been pursued by a
great variety of organizations; universities, school boards,
the Workers' Educational Association, trade unions,
churches, and bodies like the YMCA and the Women's
Institutes. Co-operation between these various bodies,
whether at the provincial or local level, has been informal
rather than systematically organized. Many government
departments—Agriculture and Education in particular—
have encouraged local and even regional efforts, but until
1947, with the establishment of the Community Programs Branch, there was little evidence of governmental
concern on a province-wide basis. The inclusion of the
words, "further education," in the title of one of the
Department of Education's three superintendents is only
one of a number of signs that a new approach is about to
be adopted. Another is the specific inclusion of adult education within the terms of reference of the colleges of
applied arts and technology.

Organization and Control, 1867-1966

One unique feature of the Ontario educational system that has not been dealt with in the preceding chapter is the existence of a governmental department with specific responsibility for higher education in the province. Ontario is the only province in Canada with a Department of University Affairs, and its Minister of University Affairs is the only member of a Canadian cabinet whose duties are exclusively centred on the development of higher education. There is no American state which has a comparable department. If one seeks a parallel one must go to the USSR.

Mention of the Department of University Affairs brings us to the whole question of the way in which education is organized and controlled by Government and here too the element of historical development is important. Indeed it is so important that it deserves a chapter of its own. In my Introduction I said that the basic problem in Ontario education is the problem of co-ordination, and in my Conclusion I shall argue that unless this problem is solved the whole system will be in danger of breaking down. Co-ordination involves the interaction of the various governmental departments concerned with related educational activities, but it also involves the interaction of individual government departments with the local authorities with which it shares responsibility; the Department of Education with local school boards, the Department of University Affairs with individual universities, the Department of Health with individual hospitals, the Department of Agriculture with the principal and staff of each of its schools. To see this general problem in correct perspective, it is necessary to understand how the present governmental organization has evolved.

THE ORGANIZATION OF THE DEPARTMENT OF EDUCATION, 1867–1966

In 1867 the staff of the Education Department consisted of a chief superintendent at a salary of $4,000, a deputy superintendent ($2,200), a senior clerk and accountant ($1,200), a clerk in charge of statistics ($1,000), a clerk in charge of correspondence ($900), an assistant clerk ($500), and a messenger ($365). There was also a grammar school inspector in the person of George Paxton Young, and there were two hundred and sixty-nine local superintendents of common schools who submitted regular reports to the department. The latter were more often than not clergymen for whom this was a part-time job, but Young was employed full-time. The chief superintendent reported to the Government and to the Legislature through the provincial secretary, who was a member of the cabinet. He was also responsible to the Council of Public Instruction. This was a body of "not more than nine persons"—of which he was an *ex officio* member—which had been established in 1846 to advise the superintendent and the Government on matters of educational policy. The council was authorized "to make such Regulations . . . as it shall deem expedient for the Organization, Government and Discipline of Common Schools," and "to examine and at its discretion recommend or disapprove of Text Books for the use of schools"; and it had rather specific responsibility for the Normal School, which had come into being after its own establishment. In all such matters the work was actually done by the chief superintendent and his staff. The council was in fact an advisory board, and it had been so described for the first four years of its existence.[1]

At this juncture, then, the Chief Superintendent, Egerton Ryerson, had the responsibility both for administering the activities of his department and for proposing policy. If a new measure was to be introduced, he had to persuade both the central and the local authorities of its merits. Convincing the central authority meant presenting the case to the Council of Public Instruction, to individual members of the Government (most notably, the Premier) and ultimately, through the provincial secretary, to the Legislature. Convincing the local authorities also implied convincing the Legislature since its members were the direct representatives of the people. But Ryerson took especial pains to bring his proposals to the attention of the local community *before* they were presented to the Legislature. He did this regularly through the agency of his annual reports and the monthly issues of the *Journal of Education*, both of which were widely distributed. He also periodically took his proposals to the people in person. On five occasions (1847, 1853, 1860, 1866, and 1869) he toured the whole province for the purpose of holding public discussion of impending legislation.

With the retirement of Ryerson in 1876, both the Council of Public Instruction and the office of the Chief Superintendent were abolished. The council's functions were assigned to the Education Department and the duties of the superintendent were assumed by a minister of the Crown. The newly created Minister of Education was also to be the head of the Education Department, with responsibility for day-to-day operation assigned to a deputy minister.

The first Minister of Education was the Hon. Adam Crooks, who had been a member of the Government since 1871 as Attorney-General and Provincial Treasurer. That he interpreted the minister's role as an active one can be seen from this passage from his first *Annual Report*:

> In February 1876, I was charged . . . with the duties of this Office, and by visits to Teachers' Associations and conferences and public meeting with municipal and school officials in more than 20 of the Counties of the Province [there were 32], I was enabled during the past year to gain such practical knowledge of the educational system under my charge as to submit to the Legislature at its session in 1877 amendments to the Law in several material particulars which were required to meet the wants of the Public and High Schools, as well as to supplement the deficiencies of the Normal Schools . . . in supplying all schools with trained teachers.[2]

Crooks was Minister for eight years, though for the final two he was largely inactive owing to serious ill health; and during this period a number of important new departures were entered upon—invariably at his instigation.

The role of the minister in *directing* educational policy was even more emphatic during the regime (1883–99) of his successor, the Hon. George W. Ross, and since Ross moved on to the premiership, in effect, to 1905. Before he had entered politics in 1872, Ross, who was a graduate of the Normal School, had been a public school teacher and inspector, and he regarded himself with some justification as a professional educator. He was also a strong and power-ful personality, a man who, like Egerton Ryerson, tended to dominate any organization with which he was connected. It is likely that Ross would have been the directing force in the Education Department no matter who had been his deputy, but the fact that the Deputy Minister was J. George

Hodgins made this almost inevitable. Hodgins, who had been Ryerson's Deputy Superintendent, entered upon his duties in 1876 fresh from the experience of having spent thirty years carrying out someone else's orders. Furthermore, he was not himself a teacher and made no pretence of being a professional educator. He was, however, an able administrator and he performed the functions assigned to him under Crooks and Ross from 1876 until 1890 with the same kind of efficiency that had marked his service under Ryerson. His successor, Alexander Marling, who had been the Chief Clerk and Accountant in 1867, was another long-time employee of the department, and also lacked professional experience. Marling died within the year, and his successor, who continued in office until his death in 1905, was John Millar.

Millar was a man of wide experience in both the public and secondary schools—at the time of his appointment he had been principal of the St. Thomas Collegiate Institute for fifteen years—and he might have been expected to provide the Minister of Education with authoritative advice about educational policy, but by this time the role of the deputy minister *vis-à-vis* the minister had been defined, and it was the minister, and not the deputy, who was the professional authority. As the obituary notice of Millar in the 1905 *Annual Report* rather plaintively states, "from that time [1890] his work was official and executive."

The Ross government was defeated at the polls in 1905 and one of the first actions of the Whitney government which succeeded it was to reorganize the Department of Education completely. The office of Superintendent was revived, for a reason that was clearly stated, "to afford the Department the constant assistance of professional experience and knowledge disassociated from the full administrative control which remains in the hands of the responsible Minister."[8]

Two major appointments were made in 1906, John Seath as Superintendent and A. H. U. Colquhoun as Deputy Minister. Seath had been a high school inspector since 1884; Colquhoun had been a journalist since his graduation from McGill in 1885, but his administrative abilities had been drawn to the attention of the Whitney government through his work as secretary of the Royal Commission on the University of Toronto, which it had appointed in 1905. Quite clearly, the intention was to provide the Minister of Education with *two* advisers, one a professional educator who would be concerned with developing educational policy, one an administrator who would see that the policies of the department once decided were efficiently carried out.

The 1906 reorganization of the department also called for the establishment of an Advisory Council of Education "as a practical method for bringing the Minister of Education in close touch with the teaching profession and enabling him, whenever he desires, to seek in a regular and systematic way the counsel and opinions of the various ranks of educationists."[4] The council was to be an elected body on which would sit representatives of the universities, the high schools, the public and separate schools, the inspectors, and school trustees. The superintendent would sit on it as the minister's representative and he would be the medium through which its recommendations were forwarded to the minister. This council was duly formed in 1906 but it never assumed importance. It was abolished in 1915.

A probable reason for the failure of the Advisory Council to play the role envisaged for it was the fact that the Superintendent was John Seath who, like Ryerson and Ross, was a very strong personality, and who was a good deal more interested in developing his own ideas than in listening to the ideas of others. It was Seath rather than the Minister or the Deputy Minister, who dominated Ontario education for the next fifteen years, and it was not by any means to everyone's dismay that with his death in 1919 the office of superintendent was again abolished. By this time the staff of the Department of Education included a number of departmental heads—Inspector of Public Libraries (since 1882), Registrar (1890s), Inspector of Manual Training and Household Science (1901), Chief Public and Separate School Inspector (1909),[5] Director of Industrial and Technical Education (1912), and Inspector of Elementary Agricultural Education (1911). Three new positions were established in 1919: Director of Professional (Teacher) Training, Inspector of Auxiliary Classes, and Provincial School Attendance Officer. For the next four years these people carried on the work of the department with the deputy minister—Colquhoun continued to occupy this position—as the co-ordinator. In 1923, the Superintendent's position was revived again, this time under the title of Chief Director. The appointee was F. W. Merchant, who had done such excellent work for ten years as Director of Industrial Education. Merchant reached retirement age in 1930, but continued for four years as a Chief Adviser to the Minister. George F. Rogers was appointed Chief Director in his place in 1930 but with the accession of the Hepburn Government in 1934 reverted to High School Inspector. This was the year that Colquhoun retired as Deputy Minister. He was replaced by Duncan McArthur, until then a professor of history at Queen's University, who a few months later also became Chief Director. Then in 1940, to make matters even more confusing, McArthur was appointed Minister of Education, and Rogers came back as Deputy Minister. It is not surprising, therefore, that the Drew government on assuming office in 1943 decided that it was time to return to the organization of 1906, which had clearly distinguished between responsibility for administration and for educational policy. The latter would be the concern of a chief director, the former of a deputy minister. Rogers was continued as Deputy Minister and J. G. Althouse was appointed Chief Director.

This at least was the division of labour outlined in an organization chart of the department which appeared in the 1944 *Annual Report* and which is reproduced as Chart 3, but within two years the attempt to separate administration from educational policy in the interests of permitting the chief director to concentrate upon professional problems had apparently failed, for the organization chart which appeared in the 1946 *Annual Report* (Chart 4) places the chief director *above* the deputy minister. In graphic terms at least, the result is tidier; whether it is as sound an arrangement in theory is a matter which can be argued, but not proved.

Both charts reveal how complex the organization of the Department of Education had become in the half century since the 1890s when its staff consisted of less than twenty people.[6] It became far more complex in the 1950s and 1960s with the enormous increase in school enrolments which followed the rising birth rate and the heavy immigration of the post-war period and with the development of post-secondary education. By 1956 it had become necessary to have not one but *two* deputy ministers. The division of duties between them is foreseen in the 1944 organizational chart where the two officers directly beneath the chief director are superintendents of elementary and secondary education. Between 1956 and 1964 one deputy minister was mainly concerned with the elementary schools, the other with the secondary; responsibility for teacher training was divided and responsibility for technical and adult education was not clear. The reorganization of 1965 (see Chart 1) introduces an entirely new structure: minister, single deputy minister, assistant deputy ministers in charge of (*a*) elementary, secondary, and teacher training *combined*; (*b*) all

CHART 3
Organization, Department of Education, 1944

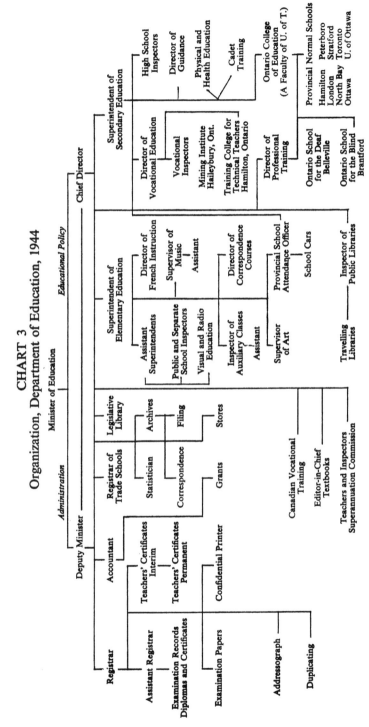

SOURCE: Ontario, Department of Education, *Annual Report of the Minister of Education, 1944* (Toronto, 1944), 98.

CHART 4
Organization, Department of Education, 1946

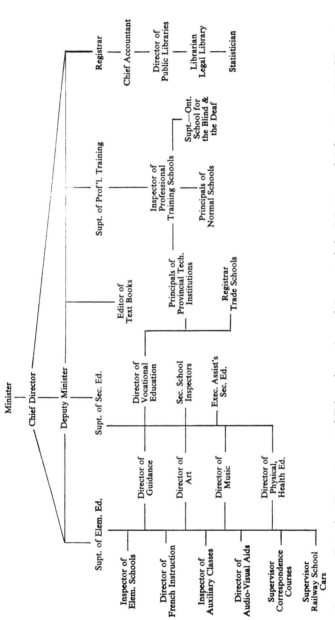

SOURCE: Ontario, Department of Education, *Annual Report of the Minister of Education, 1946* (Toronto, 1946), 98.

other education including technical and adult; and (c) administration.

The Consolidation of Local School Boards

So much for the development of the Department of Education as it has evolved in the course of a century from an organization involving a staff of eight to one which in 1965 employed several thousand. But, from the beginning, public education in Ontario has been based on a division of labour and responsibility between central and local authority. What about the development of the latter?

In 1867 local authorities were responsible either for elementary education, in which case they were elected, or for secondary education, in which case they were appointed. In urban centres, the elected trustees were responsible for all the common schools in the municipality—the public school trustees for the public schools, the separate school trustees for the separate schools—but in the rural areas, the trustees were elected by the ratepayers of a school section and had jurisdiction over a single school. For secondary education the local authority was a board appointed by either a county or a city council; for grammar school purposes cities were declared to be counties. There was also provision in 1867 for a union board of education to take care of the situation where a grammar school had "united" with one or more of the common schools in the township, village, town, or city where it was located.

Between 1865 and 1871 Egerton Ryerson made a valiant attempt to reorganize this system completely. He proposed that in the rural areas the basic unit of administration be for the elementary schools the township and for the secondary schools the county and that in the cities and towns a single board of trustees be responsible for both elementary and secondary education. He also proposed that *all* trustees be elected. But despite his efforts none of these proposals was incorporated in the legislation adopted at the end of this period. The Common School Act of 1870 permitted the consolidation of school sections into township boards but did not make this mandatory, while the Grammar School Act of 1871, which in so many other respects was revolutionary, accepted the status quo so far as public control of the schools was concerned. In the cities and towns there continued to be one board for the public schools and another for the high schools, secondary school trustees continued to be appointed, and no clear-cut system was outlined for the organization of secondary education in the rural areas.

Between 1900 and 1944 the province did gradually adopt Ryerson's proposal for the consolidation of elementary and secondary education in the cities and towns. A Board of Education Act of 1903 authorized the consolidation of elementary and secondary education under a single board for cities of one hundred thousand (at that time applicable only to Toronto), but in the following year the privilege was extended to all cities and towns and even to villages.[7] During the next four decades almost all cities and towns with four outstanding exceptions adopted this arrangement. The exceptions were Cornwall, North Bay, Ottawa, and Sudbury, each of which had—and has—a substantial French-speaking population. With the intensification of the campaign, begun in 1944 to develop district high schools, there was some reduction in the number of boards responsible for both elementary and secondary schooling because in some centres the local high school became a district high school and thus was detached from the local public schools. In 1965 there were fifty-three boards of education in Ontario. Eleven of these were in Metropolitan Toronto and were for certain purposes embraced within the Metropolitan School Board.[8]

Until the launching of an experiment in 1944 in Essex

County there were no district high schools in Ontario in the full sense of the term. The children in the rural areas attended the elementary school in their section, which in some cases extended to Grade 10, and then went to the nearest high or continuation school for their secondary education. The county council paid the school for this service; it had no school of its own. Clearly this meant that the type of programme offered in the secondary school was only incidentally designed with the particular needs of the rural community in mind. It was to provide a proper programme for this group, and *incidentally* to establish a community centre for the adults, that the Department of Education at long last began actively to promote the establishment of district high schools. The campaign has been successful. Today the entire populated area of the province is divided into high school districts and there are no less than one hundred and seventy district high school boards. The district is not, however, coterminous with the county, and to this extent Ryerson's proposal is still unfulfilled. Nor are the trustees of district high school boards elected.

Ryerson's other proposal—that school sections be abolished and the township made the basic unit of administration for the elementary schools of the rural area—was adopted eighty-eight years after his retirement with the proclamation on May 7, 1964 of Bill 54, which provided for the organization of townships and small urban municipalities (population of less than one thousand or a resident school population of less than a hundred, as township school areas). When Bill 54 came into effect on January 1st, 1965, the number of public school boards in the rural areas was reduced from 1,850 to 423 and the number of urban boards from 258 to 182.

In justice it must be added that Bill 54 was the final step in a movement which had been underway since at least the turn of the century. Particularly in the 20s and the late 50s there were strenuous efforts by the Department of Education to encourage school sections to consolidate. There was a time when there were 5,747 school sections in Ontario, most of them operating a one-room school. Almost 4,000 of these had been consolidated by the time Bill 54 completed the process.

THE ESTABLISHMENT OF THE DEPARTMENT OF UNIVERSITY AFFAIRS

Until 1951 the Ontario government found it unnecessary to adopt any mechanism for dealing with the universities of the province. Since 1901 the Legislature had been making annual grants to the University of Toronto and since 1915 to Queen's and Western. These grants were in part statutory, i.e., they continued from year to year, and in any event, since the amounts were relatively small (in 1950, $500,000 to each of Queen's and Western, approximately $4 million to Toronto), the matter could be handled by the premier's office after discussion with the representatives of each institution. But between 1948 and 1950 three other universities —Carleton, Ottawa, and McMaster—also became eligible to receive grants. Late in 1951, R. C. Wallace, who had recently retired as Principal of Queen's, was appointed a part-time consultant on university affairs. It was officially stated at that time that it had become "expedient to establish a closer liaison between the Government and the Universities of Ontario with a view to greater co-ordination of university work and to provide for the advising of the Government upon the manner of distribution of the Provincial and Federal Grants."[9] Principal Wallace died in 1956 by which time, with the addition of Assumption (now Windsor) and Waterloo, the number of institutions had

risen to eight and the total annual grant to $20 million.
Wallace's role was taken over first by Dr. J. G. Althouse,
the Chief Director of the Department of Education, then on
his sudden death late in 1956, by a cabinet minister, the
Hon. Dana Porter, Provincial Treasurer. But almost immediately the matter of advising the Government about the
universities was assigned to a committee of senior civil
servants composed of the Chief Director of Education, who
acted as chairman, the Comptroller of Finance, the Provincial Auditor, and the Deputy Minister of Economics and
Development, with an official from the Department of
Education acting as secretary, and a retired university professor acting as adviser.

By 1961 the number of institutions had risen to eleven
and the amount of the grants to over $35 million, and at
this point the Government appointed an Advisory Committee on University Affairs which was "empowered to study
all matters concerning the establishment, development,
operation, expansion and financing of the universities of
the Province."[10] The original chairman of the committee
was Mr. John Robarts, then Minister of Education, and
the other five members were the Deputy Minister of Economics, the Chief Justice of Ontario, and three business
men. When Mr. Robarts became premier in 1962, his place
on the committee was taken by his predecessor, Mr. Leslie
Frost. In September 1964 the committee's membership was
almost doubled with the addition of five persons who either
were or had been university professors. Earlier in 1964 the
Government had established a Department of University
Affairs, and the committee was now made advisory not to
the Government but to the Minister of University Affairs,
a portfolio assumed by Mr. W. G. Davis, who had succeeded
Mr. Robarts as Minister of Education. The Secretary of the
Advisory Committee was appointed Deputy Minister of
University Affairs but continued on as Secretary. In 1965

the grants to fourteen chartered universities exceeded $150 million.

The Universities Organize

While all this was going on, the universities also began to organize themselves. Oddly enough, prior to 1962 the only association the individual universities of Ontario had with each other or with any government department was through the membership that some, but not all, of them had in the University Matriculation Board, a body which had been reorganized in 1919 to include representatives of the Department of Education and which, for the past forty-five years, has exercised general supervision of the combined matriculation and departmental examinations, through the Registrar's Branch of the department. In March 1962, the Committee on University Affairs called together the presidents of all the universities which were in receipt of Government grants with a view to obtaining their reaction to a statistical report, prepared by Professor R. W. B. Jackson at the committee's request, which showed projected undergraduate enrolment in the province for the next eight years. On the adjournment of this meeting the presidents assembled by themselves, and the Committee of Presidents of the Provincially Assisted Universities and Colleges of Ontario was born. It now consists of the executive heads of Brock, Carleton, Guelph, Lakehead, Laurentian, McMaster, Ottawa, Queen's, Toronto, Trent, Waterloo, Western, Windsor, and York Universities. Waterloo Lutheran, a denominational institution which is not eligible for provincial grants, is not represented.

The Committee of Presidents has no legal status as a body officially representing the universities of the province, but it has acted in this capacity *vis-à-vis* the Ontario government for the past four years. It has published four major reports and has submitted more than a dozen memoranda to the Government on a wide range of subjects. Until recently the Committee of Presidents has had no secretariat; it has worked through committees appointed from the staffs of the member institutions. As of July 1st, 1966 a small secretariat was established. It is headed by Dr. E. F. Sheffield who, as its Executive Vice-Chairman, will devote two-thirds of his time to the work of the committee.

There has also been in existence since June 1963 the Ontario Council of University Faculty Associations, a body which represents the views of the teaching staff associations of all the universities of Ontario including Waterloo Lutheran. Like the Committee of Presidents, the Ontario Council has on a number of occasions presented its views on university matters to the Government.

A provincial student organization has also evolved in recent years. The Ontario Region of the Canadian Union of Students (ORCUS) began to meet separately from the national organization in 1964. It includes the student associations of all institutions eligible for membership in the Canadian Union of Students. ("The student association of each institution of post-secondary learning . . . that has more than 100 students represented by a democratically constituted student association.") In September 1965, an office was established in Toronto, with a full-time executive-secretary. At the annual meeting in January 1966 it was decided that in future the president would be paid to work full-time during his year in office. ORCUS also on occasion presents its views on university matters to the Government. In June 1966, the Minister of University Affairs received a brief concerning financial aid to Ontario university students presented jointly by the Committee of Presidents, the Ontario Council of University Faculty Associations, and the Ontario Region of the Canadian Union of Students.

LIAISON BETWEEN GOVERNMENT DEPARTMENTS

There neither is nor ever has been much in the way of a formal relationship between the Department of Education and the other government departments—no interlocking directorates, few standing committees, and only occasional official conferences. This is not to say that the departments have been working at cross-purposes or that there either has been or is a lack of co-operation on matters of mutual concern. The relationship has usually been close, but it has been informal rather than official and based on contact between individuals rather than on recognized procedures which follow automatically. It is an arrangement which is better geared to the solution of particular problems than to the consideration of over-all policy.

The closest relationship is with the three departments which arrange for the Department of Education to provide instruction for their educational programmes—Provincial Secretary and Citizenship (classes for new Canadians), Labour (apprenticeship programme), and Reform Institutions. Here there is literally day-to-day contact. Nonetheless the recent establishment by Education and Labour of an Interdepartmental Committee on Technical and Trades Training for the purpose of developing policies and procedures to ensure that technical and trades training programmes are in keeping with the needs and demands of the province's rapidly developing industrialized economy is a new departure. The only interdepartmental committee involving Education and the other two departments (and also Health) is the School Management Committee, a body which arranges salary contracts for teachers in schools operated directly by government departments.

With the departments which conduct or supervise their own schools, the relationship to the Department of Education is less close at both the official and the informal level. Almost the only link with Lands and Forests is the membership of a senior official of the Department of Education on the Advisory Council of the Forest Ranger School. There is a similar link with Health; another senior official is a member of the Educational Advisory Committee to the College of Nurses which is responsible for the training of nurses. For many years the Chief Director of Education was a member of the Board of Governors of the Ontario Agricultural College, but with the establishment of the University of Guelph this link has been cut. At the informal level the local secondary school inspectors maintain close liaison with the agricultural schools at Kemptville and Ridgetown. There are representatives of the Department of Health on certain of the Department of Education's curriculum committees. A representative of the Department of Education has been appointed to the Planning Council on Nursing Education and Related Matters which the Minister of Health established early in 1965.

Since over 90 per cent of the system is supervised by the Departments of Education and University Affairs, the relations between these two departments are obviously of high importance. Technically there is no relationship. It happens that at the present time (September 1966) the same person is the minister of both departments but this, of course, need not necessarily be the case. It happens, too, that both the Deputy Minister and the Assistant Deputy Minister of the Department of University Affairs were in the Department of Education prior to their present appointments and one can assume that their contacts with the senior officials in the Department of Education are wide ranging and close. But again the situation rests on chance: there is no guarantee that such appointments will always bring to the Department of University Affairs persons with Department of Education experience.

The most encouraging development of 1966 has been the introduction of formal arrangements to insure the co-ordination of the activities of the departments of Health and University Affairs in the health sciences field. In February the Ministers of Health and University Affairs held a joint meeting with the representatives of the five universities (McMaster, Ottawa, Queen's, Toronto, Western Ontario) engaged in the health sciences—medicine, dentistry, nursing, pharmacy, physical and occupational therapy, public health or hygiene, medical social work, clinical psychology, dietetics, speech therapy, and audiology. The purpose of this meeting was to acquaint the universities with Government plans for the development of health resources and manpower in Ontario. There were two very practical consequences. The first was the establishment of a Senior Co-ordinating Committee, consisting of the Deputy Ministers of the Departments of Health and University Affairs and the Chairman of the Ontario Hospital Services Commission, whose task it would be to review the plans and needs of each university and to develop a co-ordinated plan for the development of the health sciences in Ontario. The second result of this meeting was the establishment of the Ontario Council of Health. Such a council was proposed at the February meeting and established by the Minister of Health in April. Its seventeen members include the Deputy Minister of Health as Chairman, the Chairman of the Ontario Hospital Services Commission, four persons representing medicine, dentistry, pharmacy, and nursing, one person representing the hospitals, five persons representing public groups (for example, labour), and five persons appointed directly by the government for their expert knowledge in particular fields. The Ontario Council of Health is to be the senior advisory body on health matters to the Minister of Health and the Government of Ontario and its specific terms of reference are the following:

(*a*) the co-ordination of health services with an emphasis on co-operation and active participation of key agencies, associations and groups interested in health arrangements;

(*b*) techniques for long-term planning which are sufficiently flexible to accommodate short-term projects and deal with urgent situations;

(*c*) priorities and phasing;

(*d*) health resources development and maintenance, including the health resources required for education and training, services and research;

(*e*) health manpower requirements;

(*f*) such other matters as the council may deem to be pertinent to the objectives set out above; and,

(*g*) any specific subjects referred to the council by the Minister of Health.

A research and planning branch within the Department of Health has been established to supply the council with the information it will need to carry out its tasks.

Conclusion

There are two questions to be answered when one attempts to evaluate an educational system. The first is whether it provides the full range of educational facilities that are needed to sustain and develop the economy and the cultural tradition of the jurisdiction which the system is designed to serve. Here one is concerned with an examination of the separate parts of the system: are there, for example, a sufficient number of secondary schools (or medical schools or public libraries) and is the secondary school programme one which provides adequately for the needs of the secondary school population? The second question centres upon the relation of the separate parts of the system to each other, of the secondary school programme to the elementary school programme on one hand and on the other to the programmes of the various post-secondary institutions to which high school graduates proceed. Is the system so structured that its various parts function effectively as individual units but also in co-ordination with each other? In the pursuit of an answer to this question one is concerned with organizational structure and with the means adopted to decide upon and to implement policy.

In the case of the Ontario educational system the answer

to the first of these two questions is—at first glance—yes. The system does contain all the educational elements that are required to provide for the needs of any of its citizens. Somewhere in the province one can find every conceivable type of institution and somewhere one can find every conceivable type of educational service. Provision is made for the physically or mentally handicapped, for the geographically remote, for those whose native language is not English, for those who cannot afford the costs of the education or the training they seek. One can without leaving Ontario become a plumber or a nuclear physicist, an artist or an investment counsellor, an expert on diesel engines or on the giraffe.

It would, of course, be surprising if this were not the case. Ontario is both a populous and a relatively rich jurisdiction and it has therefore enough people and enough resources to develop all the institutions and all the services that an industrialized society requires. One could certainly make the same statement of at least two other Canadian provinces and of probably a dozen American states. But, the question can be put in other ways: Are all the facilities required provided in sufficient quantity and in a sufficient number of locations to make it relatively easy for most people in the province to take advantage of them? Are there enough institutions of the various kinds and are the various special services in fact available to the majority of those who require them? There is also the matter of quality. It is small consolation to know that there are ten excellent high schools in Ontario if it is also known that there are several hundred others which are substandard.

The first of these sub-questions—the quantitative one—can, I think, be answered affirmatively. There are certainly enough elementary schools, secondary schools, teachers' colleges, schools of nursing, universities, and public libraries, and they are on the whole geographically well-

placed. Indeed it could be argued that in each case a reduction in the total numbers would, in the short run at least,
be beneficial since some of the existing units are too small
to offer an adequate programme. In 1965–6 there were not
a sufficient number of institutes of technology but there
obviously will be when the nineteen colleges of applied
arts and technology that have been proposed have been
established.

With regard to special schools and special services, it is
difficult to make any judgment, principally because the
precise needs of the province in these areas have never
systematically been surveyed. But, one has the impression
that if it is demonstrated that there is a need for a second
Art College in Ontario, or two more agricultural schools,
or for a dozen more railway classroom cars, it or they will
be provided.

I have no intention of making any judgments about the
quality of the component parts of the Ontario educational
system; this is probably beyond the competence of any one
person and it is certainly beyond mine. Rather I shall
content myself with citing evidence which indicates that,
in the opinion of those most responsible for education in
Ontario, notably the Minister of Education and his chief
advisers, there is room for improvement at all levels.

During the past three years the Minister of Education has
appointed three major committees to study and report on
basic areas of the Ontario educational system. One of these
—the Committee on the Training of Elementary School
Teachers, chaired by C. R. MacLeod—we have already
referred to at some length. Since the recommendations of
the MacLeod Committee call for an almost complete change
in the arrangements for training teachers for the elementary
schools, it can be taken for granted that the existing arrangements are not satisfactory.

We have also referred in passing to another committee

which the Minister appointed in 1964—the Grade 13
Study Committee, whose chairman was F. A. Hamilton,
Director of Education for the City of Guelph. Its terms of
reference were:

> . . . to inquire into and report upon the nature and function of
> the Grade 13 year in the Ontario educational system particularly
> in the light of opinions expressed frequently by responsible
> persons that, despite the fact that much can be said in its favour,
> (*a*) Grade 13 is a cram year with too much emphasis upon
> the memorization of factual information and upon the prepara-
> tion for the final Departmental examination;
> (*b*) the year should provide a richer educational experience
> than it does for all students whether they proceed to universities
> and other institutions of higher learning or directly to some
> form of employment, and
> (*c*) the year should be a better liaison between the school
> programme and the programmes of universities and other insti-
> tutions of higher learning.

This committee submitted its report in June 1964, four
months after its appointment, and an enormous amount of
time has been spent during the subsequent two years by a
large number of people in the Department of Education and
in the schools and universities in the implementation of its
thirty-seven recommendations. Most of these recommendations bore on the Grade 13 year itself and have resulted in
substantial changes in its curriculum and in the manner in
which instruction is provided and progress evaluated. But
the committee also made one recommendation that was only
indirectly related to Grade 13 and it made one proposal
that concerned all the grades of both the elementary and
secondary school. The recommendation was for the establishment of community colleges. These were proposed in
order to provide a proper alternative to Grade 13 for Grade
12 graduates; and this recommendation has been implemented by the legislation establishing colleges of applied
arts and technology. The proposal, which was not forma-

lized in a specific recommendation, was that the elementary and secondary programmes be provided in twelve years of schooling with the Grade 13 (or matriculation) year being offered in Grade 12. The intention was not to abolish Grade 13 in the sense that its course of study would be removed from the secondary school but to rearrange the course of study from Grade 1 through to Grade 11 so that the students entering the matriculation year would have attained, at the end of Grade 11, the standard now attained at the end of Grade 12. The committee had noted that a substantial number of students entering the universities were doing so at the age of seventeen, a situation which indicated that they had completed the thirteen grades in twelve years by "accelerating," i.e., by taking the academic work of three grades in two years, normally while attending the elementary school, and it concluded that the same result could be achieved by a revision of the curriculum in all grades, the accelerating students henceforth doing thirteen grades in twelve years rather than three in two. Perhaps because this proposal was not presented in the form of a specific recommendation, no official action has been taken on it. But the Minister of Education has made no secret of the department's interest in it, and it is known that the department's Curriculum Branch is busily engaged in the studies required for its adoption. This suggests that there is room for improvement in the elementary and secondary schools.

The third committee initiated by the Minister is the Committee on the Aims and Objectives of Education in the Schools of Ontario, under the chairmanship of Mr. Justice Emmett Hall. Appointed in April 1965, its terms of reference suggest that its first concern is with kindergarten and the first six grades, but since the committee has been asked "to set forth the aims of education for the educational system of the Province," there is nothing to prevent and

much to recommend it moving on to the secondary school
and beyond. The appointment of such a committee is hardly
consistent with the view that the educational system of
Ontario is working perfectly, and pending the publication
of its report, which is not expected until at least the summer
of 1967, there is further reason to assume that there is room
for improvement in the elementary and secondary schools
as well as in the teachers' colleges, the institutes of technology, and Grade 13. Nor can the situation of the universities be regarded with complacency. Both the Committee of
Presidents and the Ontario Council of University Faculty
Associations have approved the recommendation of the
Presidents' Research Committee in "From the Sixties to the
Seventies: An Appraisal of Higher Education in Ontario"
that they jointly request the Minister of University Affairs
to authorize a commission under the sponsorship of the
Committee on University Affairs and the Committee of
Presidents to study the existing pattern of higher education
in Ontario (including the colleges of applied arts and technology) and to make recommendations for its development,
integration, and governance.

The truth of the matter is that almost every aspect of
the Ontario educational system is undergoing very close
scrutiny. This large-scale self-study has not adopted the
form of a single Royal Commission and its actuality therefore is less obvious than the comparable self-study that has
recently been undertaken by the province of Quebec. But
actual this self-study is, and underlying it is the conviction
that none of the component parts of the Ontario educational
system is working as efficiently as circumstance demands.

The advantages of a single all-embracing study are that
nothing presumably is overlooked and everything is examined in relation to everything else. The Parent Commission examined everything, objectives, curriculum, finance,
control, every level of education, every type of institution,

and the structure of the system itself. Ontario's approach is of the piecemeal variety—separate studies of particular problems. As an approach this too has advantages; it is less costly, it takes less time, it leads to quicker results. The danger is that something will be overlooked, and the element in an educational system which is most likely to be overlooked is its own inner structure. But this is to bring us to our second question: Is the educational system of Ontario so structured that its various parts function effectively as individual units but also in co-ordination with each other? To at least the second part of this question the answer unquestionably is no. While it is probably true to say that on the whole the individual units do function effectively as units, there is a good deal of evidence that they operate as units rather than as organic parts of a larger complex.

Thus, there is the fact that in many localities responsibility for elementary education rests with two types of school board (the public and the separate school) and responsibility for secondary education with a third; this can hardly be said to encourage a unified attack on the problems of education at these two obviously interlocking levels. Next, the relationship between the secondary schools and the various post-secondary institutions to which the Grade 12 and Grade 13 graduates proceed—the teachers' colleges, the hospital schools of nursing, the institutes of technology, the universities—is a very loose one, and is one which is more marked by the exchange of official transcripts and form letters than by the vivid exchange of ideas and the interaction of personality. Relatively few people from these post-secondary institutions visit the high schools in their area and relatively few high school people visit the post-secondary institutions to which their students proceed; of those who do, in both cases the majority are administrators rather than teachers. There is a similar lack of coming and going between the various post-secondary institutions, and there is no organization of any kind at either the provincial or local level which draws together representatives of all of them and of the secondary schools for the discussion of problems of mutual concern. The isolation of the teachers' colleges from the universities is particularly noticeable even though the policy of locating teachers' colleges on or adjacent to university campuses has been developed by the Department of Education in recent years; a more organic relationship than that provided by geographic propinquity is clearly needed and is in fact proposed by the MacLeod Report. It is also apparent that the various government departments active in the education field have given inadequate attention to the combining of their efforts or the pooling of their resources. Was it really necessary to wait until 1965 to begin the experiment of involving the institutes of technology in the training of nurses and of social workers? Is there no place for agriculture in a technical institute?

One of the characteristics of the Ontario educational system is that it is thoroughly compartmentalized. Our review of the system, as it revealed itself in 1965–6 demonstrates this clearly, and our review of its historical development provides the explanation that there has been a general failure over the years to recognize that all parts of the system are in an almost literal sense interlocking and hence that no one of them can be changed without all the others being affected. Change the elementary school curriculum in any way and all the blocks which rise upon it must be realigned; equally, alter the arrangements for the training of teachers at the universities or in the teachers' colleges and it becomes necessary to readjust the elementary school curriculum. There will be no marked improvement of the Ontario educational system—and probably some deterioration—unless this obvious fact is so thoroughly recognized that it becomes the accepted first principle in all educational decisions.

Acceptance of the principle that all activities are inter-related would lead to two quite different kinds of reorganization. The first would chiefly affect the individual departments of the government. In the case of the Department of Education it would involve a closer relationship between its various branches; in the case of the other departments, it would involve a closer relationship with each other and with the Department of Education. This is a direction in which the province is already moving. The second kind of reorganization is a much more radical step and one which apparently has never been seriously considered. *This is to organize education, at all levels throughout the province, on a regional basis.*

But first a few remarks about the reorganization that is already in train. There are many signs that the several departments are moving away from what might be called departmental separatism. The new organization of the Department of Education is designed among other things to eliminate the barriers that have separated the elementary from the secondary schools; responsibility for all instruction from kindergarten to Grade 13 is assigned to a single assistant deputy minister. It is also designed to co-ordinate adult education with technological and professional training; hence an Assistant Deputy Minister in charge of Provincial Schools *and* Further Education. The proposed new Grade 13 is intended to facilitate the transition from high school to university by making the matriculation year once again what it was originally intended to be, the equivalent of a first-year university course. The colleges of applied arts and technology will take over the role of the institutes of technology but they will also be adult education centres. Provision is to be made for able students to transfer from these colleges to the universities. There is to be a more intimate relationship between the Ontario colleges of education and the universities with which they are associated than was the case from 1920 to 1965. If the MacLeod Report is implemented, the teachers' colleges will no longer be isolated from the universities and the training of elementary and secondary school teachers will no longer be separate.

Closer liaison has also been developing during the past twelve months between departments. What is mainly required here is the systematic development of a network of standing interdepartmental committees which meet regularly and whose terms of reference are sufficiently general to permit the members to consider over-all policy. The Senior Co-ordinating Committee established by the Departments of Health and University Affairs provides the model. There should be similar committees involving Education and University Affairs, Education and Agriculture, Education and Health, Education and Labour, Education, University Affairs and Labour. There should also be a committee involving all departments of the government, on which each would be represented by either the minister or the deputy minister, and this for two reasons.

First, to avoid competition between departments for slices of the provincial budget; the development of the educational system *as a whole* should be the point of reference in deciding what proportion of the provincial budget should be allocated to education and within this figure what funds should be assigned to particular departments. The second reason is also based on the facts of financial life. All negotiations with the federal government concerning financial support for education in Ontario should be based on a co-ordinated plan for the development of the system as a whole. Unless there is an opportunity for cabinet ministers to examine the whole picture, some parts of the system will be developed, others overlooked.

Co-ordination at the top, however, is not enough; what

is of far greater importance is functional co-ordination at the operational level. To achieve this in Ontario requires something more than a refinement of existing techniques. It involves a new type of structure.

If one accepts the principle that the parts of an educational system are interlocking, then it follows that the persons working in any particular part ought to be familiar with what is being done in all the others. They obviously do not require the kind of detailed knowledge of each of the other parts that they need to have of their own, but rather a clear understanding of what each of the other parts is attempting to do and of the methods it adopts to achieve its ends. There is, in Ontario at present, no organization at either the provincial, regional, or local level which is designed to produce this kind of understanding. Nor is there any organization in Ontario which is specifically concerned with the co-ordination of educational services at all levels. The lack of such organizations is one reason for the failure of the Ontario educational system to prove as effective in practice as in theory it ought to be. The parts may be interlockable, but they aren't interlocking. All the parts may be available, but does anyone know where they all are?

There are two problems here; the need to develop understanding of the different parts of the system on the part of all persons working in it, and the need to co-ordinate educational services. Obviously the problems are related; the co-ordination of services will be relatively easy to arrange if everyone understands what everyone else is doing. Consequently, one can visualize a single solution to the two problems. This is, in fact, what I propose; the establishment in Ontario of a number of regional educational councils whose function would be to develop a close relationship between the various institutions over which each had jurisdiction and to co-ordinate the educational services of the region.

The establishment of regional councils as the local authority in *educational* matters would provide a new solution to the problem of centralized and decentralized control. As it now stands the chief central authority in education, the Department of Education, is dealing with local authorities which range from the Toronto Board of Education with a total expenditure for operating purposes in 1965 of over $34 million to the Brockville Public School Section in Cochrane District which spent $7,644. It could be argued that, *vis-à-vis* the Department of Education, the Toronto Board is too powerful; certainly, *vis-à-vis* the Department of Education, the old school section and now the township board is not powerful enough. Unless the local authorities are of roughly comparable size, it is not likely that a proper balance between central and local authority can be obtained. Under the scheme proposed the regional authorities would be of similar size.

Let me illustrate what I have in mind by reference to the three districts in the northwest of the province—Kenora, Rainy River, and Thunder Bay. This is an area with a population of 257,000. It is one of the ten Economic Regions (Lakehead-Northwestern) into which the province has been divided since 1954 for purposes of economic development. It is one of the college of applied arts and technology areas (No. 18), and it is one of the fourteen library regional systems (Northwestern). Located within the region are two hundred and thirty-eight public and separate schools, eighteen secondary schools, Lakehead University, the Technical Division of Lakehead University (which is the basis for a college of applied arts and technology), the Lakehead Teachers' College, and three hospital schools of nursing. The Northwestern Library System embraces twenty-one member libraries in as many communities.

The duty of the Ontario Provincial Library Council as

specified in the recently approved Public Libraries Act is to make recommendations to the Minister of Education with respect to the co-ordination of library service in Ontario. I am suggesting that a Lakehead-Northwestern Educational Council be established whose duty would be to make recommendations to the Government of Ontario with respect to the development and co-ordination of education in this region of the province. The council ought to report to the Government of Ontario, rather than to the Minister of Education, because its terms of reference involve not one but many government departments.

I would suggest that the council should have thirty members, twenty-four of whom would be nominated by appropriate institutions or organizations: elementary schools, 6; secondary schools, 6; Lakehead University, 3; Technical Division, Lakehead University (pending establishment of a CAAT), 3; Lakehead Teachers' College, 2; hospital schools of nursing, 2; and Regional Library System, 2. These numbers would permit the inclusion of classroom teachers and professors, administrators (principals, deans, directors, president), and trustees or governors, and would provide under normal circumstances a wide range of subject matter specialization. But it is possible that the twenty-four persons thus selected would not include, for example, a scientist or a person active in the field of adult education. If the remaining six places in the council were filled by the twenty-four thus appointed, obvious gaps in the council's combined experience and predilection could be avoided.

Since the duty of the council would be to make recommendations about the development and co-ordination of education in the region, its members would have to become familiar with the work being done and the problems being confronted at all educational levels and in all types of institutions. Since the membership of the council would be drawn from all levels and would represent every type of

institution, this should not be difficult to arrange. At each
meeting of the council there could be a report from one or
more of the various branches of the system—the elementary
schools and the hospital schools of nursing one month,
Lakehead University and the Lakehead Teachers' College
the next. These reports would be reasonably brief—a half-
hour presentation—and they would be concerned not with
details but with issues, developments, possibilities, and com-
plications. Each report would be essentially an exercise in
interpretation, an effort to explain what the particular type
of school or the particular type of programme was attempting to do and wherein and for what reasons it was falling
short. Such an exercise would be of as much value to the
person or persons preparing it as for those who would be
receiving it; it would force the preparer to define the issues,
to determine the significance of the developments, to establish the feasibility of the possibilities, and to distinguish
the incidental complication from the inhibiting one. He
would know that he was not preaching to the converted and
that his case would have to be proved. But at the same time
he would know that he was among workers in the same
field and that he had only to prove his case to elicit a
sympathetic and positive response.

Provided with such reports the council would be in a
position to identify the areas of misunderstanding or ignorance which were causing friction between what ought to
be well-lubricated interlocking parts; in such cases the
remedy would be at hand in its own powers of influence. It
would also be in a position to identify missing parts. Perhaps
the facilities for the education of the hard-of-hearing are
inadequate in the Lakehead-Northwestern region or perhaps
there is a clear need for a course for dental hygienists. Here
action would take the form of recommendations to the
Government.

The council's most important function, however, would

be to develop an understanding of the system throughout the region. It would be the duty of the individual members of the council to interpret the state of education in the region to the constituency which he or she represented. It would be incumbent, for example, on the Lakehead University members of the council to report to the administration and the faculty of the university on the problems which the elementary schools or the hospital schools of nursing were facing. And similarly with the elementary school representatives; it would be their business to inform the elementary school teachers of the region about Lakehead University's actual position.

From what has been said it will be apparent that I do not see the Lakehead-Northwestern Education Council as a body which directs or controls or administers anything but its own affairs. There are dozens of excellent reasons to support the argument that control of elementary education should rest with elementary school people, with elementary school teachers, elementary school principals, and elementary school trustees; and just as many that the same situation should apply in the case of secondary schools, universities, colleges of applied arts and technology, teachers' colleges, hospital schools of nursing, public libraries, and so on. It is not the intention to have all the educational activity in the Lakehead-Northwestern Educational Region organized by, for example, Lakehead University or to have Lakehead University's affairs organized by the regional council. Nor is it the intention to encourage all potential university students of the Lakehead-Northwestern region to attend Lakehead University or all potential elementary school teachers to attend Lakehead Teachers' College. The function of the council, as I see it, is not legislative, or judicial, or administrative; rather, it is advisory in the best sense of the term.

What a Lakehead-Northwestern Educational Council

could do would be to keep consistently in the mind of all its members and through them, if they do their job properly, the thousands whom they represent the simple but easily forgotten fact that education is a continuing or continual process that has a high disregard for convenient but artificial pigeon holes. The Lakehead Teachers' College is a convenient but artificial pigeon hole. Its students—and its staff—come from other educational areas and they will move on from Lakehead Teachers' College to still others. Once this is recognized the work at Lakehead Teachers' College will be seen not as an isolated activity but as one which is an integral part, not merely of the educational system, but also of the region which it serves.

The Lakehead-Northwestern region has been cited simply for illustrative purposes. As strong an argument can be made for an educational council in the southeastern or southwestern parts of the province. The whole province, indeed, ought to be divided into educational regions and a council established for each. The problem is how to draw the boundaries.

None of the three ways in which the province is already subdivided for educational purposes is entirely satisfactory. The ten area superintendencies (see p. 14–15) produce wide variations in population (257,000 in Northwestern Ontario, 893,000 in Western Ontario) and they bear no relation to the ten economic regions of the province. Both the library regions (see p. 101) and the CAAT Areas (see p. 97) do take the economic regions into account, but there are some odd departures in the case of the Library Regions (for example, Frontenac County, which includes Kingston, is detached from the remainder of the Eastern Ontario Economic Region), and several of the CAAT Areas do not include a university or university college. It seems essential to me that the university as an institution be included in the membership of each regional council because a university today occupies such a central role in an educational system—for example, as the source of teachers for all the other institutions—that the absence of its representatives would render the answer to most questions incomplete. In the CAAT division, four areas are assigned to Metropolitan Toronto. This is a highly desirable model to follow since it divides a population of close to two million into four groups, but unfortunately it is a division which runs counter to the existing arrangement for the organization of elementary and secondary schools and also to the regional library system (Metropolitan Toronto is a single regional library system). Hence I am proposing twelve educational regions, with the qualification that one of them, Metropolitan Toronto, should be organized for certain purposes into four sub-regions (see Table 5).

I have no doubt that this particular drawing of boundaries has flaws. Certainly it can be argued that the counties of Peel and Halton on the one side and of Ontario on the other ought not to be associated with Metropolitan Toronto, that Wellington county naturally belongs with Huron, Perth, and Waterloo, and that for no purpose should one region be, in terms of population, three times larger than any other. Some distortion is inevitable if the principle of including a university or university college in each region is accepted. But I hope that serious consideration of this proposal will not be rejected simply on the grounds that the geography is unacceptable. The question is not whether these particular regional educational councils should be established but whether in the interests of education in Ontario a system of regional educational councils should be introduced. If the answer is in the affirmative, then the boundaries can be properly drawn.

I also anticipate the objection that what is here proposed is simply a proliferation of meetings and reports in each region; meetings of the full council and its various

TABLE 5
Proposed Educational Regions

Educational Region	Existing Regions				University	Post Secondary Institutions		
	Economic*	CAAT	Library System	Population†		Teacher Training	Vocational	Hospital Schools of Nursing
OTTAWA VALLEY (Carleton, Lanark, Prescott, Renfrew, Russell)	Eastern Ontario Sub-region A	Area 1	Part of Eastern Ontario Regional Library System	560,000	Carleton Ottawa	Ottawa T.C., University of Ottawa T.C.	Eastern Ontario Institute of Tech., Ottawa Vocational Centre	7 Ottawa Pembroke Renfrew
UPPER ST. LAWRENCE (Frontenac, Leeds, Grenville, Dundas, Stormont, Glengarry)	Eastern Ontario Sub-region B	Area 2	Part of Lake Ontario Regional Library System	290,000	Queen's	McArthur College of Education	Eastern Ontario School of Agriculture, Kemptville	7 Brockville Cornwall Kingston
LAKE ONTARIO (Durham, Haliburton, Hastings, Lennox & Addington, Northumberland, Peterborough, Victoria Prince Edward)	Lake Ontario Economic Region	Area 3 plus Durham from Area 4	Part of Lake Ontario Regional Library System	370,000	Trent	Peterborough T.C.		3 Belleville Peterborough
BURLINGTON (Brant and Wentworth)	Niagara Sub-region A	Area 9 less parts of Haldimand, Lincoln	South Central Regional Library System	508,000	McMaster	Hamilton T.C.	Hamilton Inst. of Technology	4 Brantford Hamilton
NIAGARA (Haldimand, Lincoln, Welland)	Niagara Sub-region B	Area 10 plus parts of Haldimand, Lincoln	Niagara Regional Library System	389,000	Brock	St. Catharines T.C.		3 St Catharines

TABLE 5—continued

| Educational Region | Existing Regions | | | | Post Secondary Institutions | | | |
	Economic*	CAAT	Library System	Population†	University	Teacher Training	Vocational	Hospital Schools of Nursing
LAKE ERIE (Elgin, Middlesex, Norfolk, Oxford)	Lake Erie Economic Region	Area 11	Lake Erie Regional Library System	437,000	Western Ontario	London T.C. Althouse College of Education	Ontario Vocational Centre, London	4 London St. Thomas Woodstock
LAKE ST. CLAIR (Essex, Kent, Lambton)	Lake St. Clair Economic Region	Areas 12 & 13	Southwestern Regional Library System	528,000	Windsor	Windsor T.C.	Western Ontario Institute of Technology, Windsor Western Ontario School of Agriculture, Ridgetown	5 Chatham Sarnia Windsor
UPPER GRAND RIVER (Huron, Perth, Waterloo)	Upper Grand River Economic Region less Wellington	Area 14 less Wellington	Midwestern Regional Library System less Wellington	313,000	Waterloo Waterloo Lutheran	Stratford T.C.		3 Kitchener Stratford
GEORGIAN BAY (Wellington, Bruce, Grey, Dufferin, Simcoe, Muskoka, Parry Sound)	Georgian Bay Economic Region plus Wellington	Area 15 plus Wellington	Parts of Georgian Bay and Algonquin Regional Library System	430,000	Guelph		Ontario Ranger School, Dorset	5 Barrie Galt Guelph Orillia
NORTHEASTERN ONTARIO (Cochrane, Nipissing, Timiskaming, Sudbury, Algoma, Manitoulin)	Northeastern Ontario Economic Region	Areas 16 & 17	Parts of North Central, North-eastern & Algonquin Regional Library System	551,000	Laurentian	North Bay T.C. Sudbury T.C.		5 Sault Ste. Marie Sudbury Timmins
LAKEHEAD-NORTH-WESTERN ONTARIO (Kenora, Rainy River, Thunder Bay)	Lakehead-Northwestern Ontario Economic Region	Area 18	Northwestern Regional Library System	257,000	Lakehead	Lakehead T.C.	Technical Division Lakehead Univ.	3 Fort William Port Arthur

TABLE 5—concluded

	Existing Regions					Post Secondary Institutions			
Educational Region	Economic*	CAAT	Library System	Population†	University	Teacher Training	Vocational	Hospital Schools of Nursing
METROPOLITAN TORONTO (Ontario, York, Halton, Peel)	Metropolitan Economic Region							
Toronto East (Ontario, Townships of Scarborough, East York)		Area 5 plus Ontario from Area 4	Parts of Metro Toronto and Central Ontario Regional Library System	491,000	Scarborough (U. of T.)		Centennial College of Applied Arts & Technology	3 Oshawa Whitby Toronto East General
Toronto North (Township of North York)		Area 7	Part of Metro Toronto Regional Library System	374,000	York			
Toronto Central (City of Toronto)		Area 19	Part of Metro Toronto Regional Library System	736,200	Toronto Ontario Institute for Studies in Education	Toronto T.C., Ontario College of Education, Toronto	Ryerson Polytechnical Institute 3 Provincial Institutes of Trade Ontario College of Art Toronto Board of Education Adult Education Centre	10
Toronto West (Halton, Peel, Townships of Etobicoke & York)		Areas 6 & 8	Parts of Metro Toronto, Central Ontario & South Central Regional Library Systems	658,600	Erindale College (U. of T.)	Lakeshore T.C.		

*For a full discussion of the economic regions of Ontario see *Ontario Survey: Economic & Social Aspects* (Toronto, 1961), 237–8.

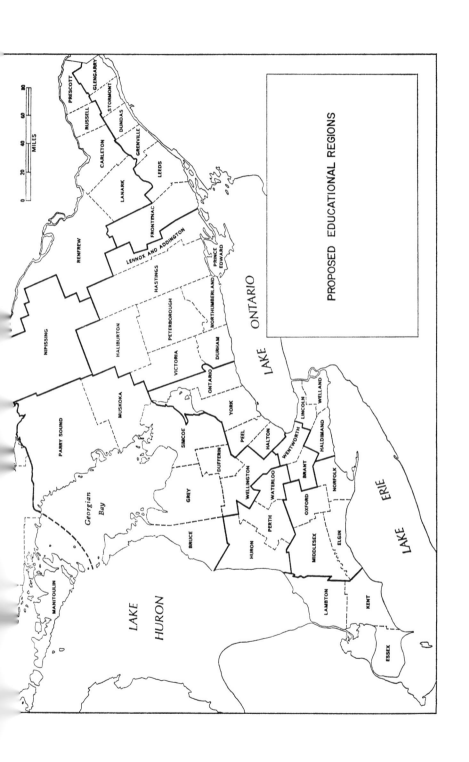

PROPOSED EDUCATIONAL REGIONS

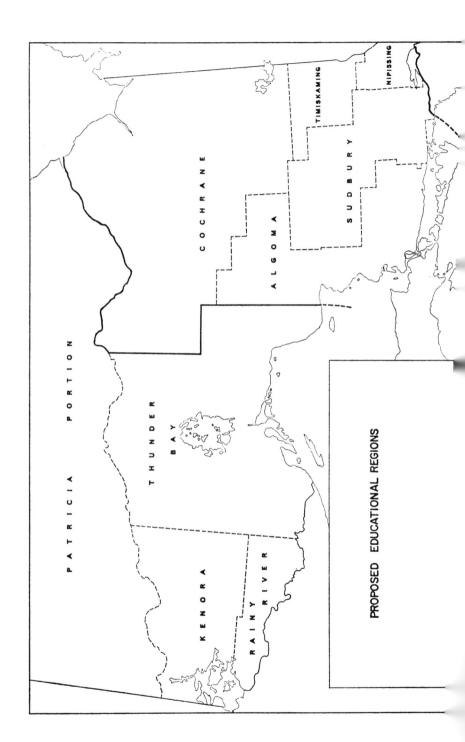

PROPOSED EDUCATIONAL REGIONS

subcommittees, meetings of elementary school teachers, secondary school teachers, etc. to elect representatives to the council and to receive reports from it, and meetings of groups of elementary and secondary school teachers or of representatives of the hospital schools of nursing and the college of applied arts and technology to pursue matters of mutual concern identified by the council. And surely there are enough committee meetings and unread reports as it is. But is this, in fact, the case? Or, is it that in each area and in each institution the same small group of people are appointed to far too many committees and that the reason so many reports are unread is that they are sent to the wrong people? At this point I can become personal, since for the past half-dozen years I have been one of the people in my particular area and institution who sits on far too many committees and who hasn't time to read the half-dozen reports which appear regularly in each week's mail. But there was a time—and not too long ago—when I wasn't on any committees at all, even though I was employed full-time as a university teacher at a reputable university. And there was a time when I would have been delighted to receive anything at all in the mail—even publishers' announcements —and when I would have given a report undivided and enthusiastic attention. It is a matter of distributing the load. One of the weaknesses of education in Ontario is that in all institutions too few people are involved in the important decisions and too many are in the position where they feel that they are simply employees. The establishment of regional educational councils would necessarily draw many teachers and professors now effectively confined to their classrooms into the corridors of power and influence.

The basic Canadian problem, as we all know, is the problem of federal-provincial relations, and most of Canadian history can be described as a search for a satisfactory division of labour between the central government in Ottawa and the governments of the provinces. The problem for each province is the same problem in the provincial context; their histories, if we disregard for the moment the running battle with Ottawa, are equally a search for a satisfactory division of labour between central government and local municipality. No doubt the problem in the municipality can be defined in similar terms. In its several guises, the problem is the fundamental problem of democratic government.

Because a democracy assumes for its effective operation an educated citizenry, its educational system is of special importance. The purpose of the system is "to provide educational opportunity so that every person . . . can realize his full potential as a human being." This is the ideal of the present Minister of Education for Ontario—the words omitted are "in Ontario," and the subject Mr. Davis was discussing (at a press conference on January 14th, 1965) was the reorganization of the department over which he presides. I suspect that a matching quotation could be drawn from statements made during the past two years by each of Mr. Davis' counterparts in the other nine Canadian provinces. His task—and theirs—is a never-ending effort to develop an organizational structure which encourages every individual within the particular province to realize his fullest potentiality.

Bibliography, Notes, Index

Bibliography

BELL, WALTER N. *The Development of the Ontario High School.* Toronto: University of Toronto Press, 1918. An historical account of developments from 1790 to 1883, chiefly of value for the account of the breakdown of the plans envisaged in the 1871 Act.

BISSELL, CLAUDE T. "Ontario" in Robin S. Harris, ed., *Changing Patterns of Higher Education in Canada.* Toronto: University of Toronto Press, 1966. An analysis of developments in higher education in the province since 1962, and a statement of current problems.

CALVIN, DELANO D. *Queen's University at Kingston, 1841–1941.* Kingston: Queen's University, 1941. The standard history of Queen's University during its first century. Fuller information about the Kingston School of Mines is provided in A. L. Clark, *The First Fifty Years: A History of the Science Faculty of Queen's University 1893–1943.* Kingston: Queen's University, 1943.

COLEMAN, HERBERT T. J. *Public Education in Upper Canada.* New York: Teachers' College, Columbia University, 1907. Still a useful study of the nineteenth century period.

Committee of Presidents of Provincially Assisted Universities and Colleges of Ontario. *Post-Secondary Education in Ontario, 1962–1970: Report of the Presidents of the Universities of Ontario to the Advisory Committee on University Affairs.* Toronto: University of Toronto Press, 1963. This and the following two reports were prepared by the Presidents' Research Committee, a group originally of eight and subsequently of ten university professors and administrators under the chairmanship from April 1962 of John J. Deutsch, Queen's University and from October 1963 until June 1966 of R. B. Willis, University of Western Ontario.

———. *The Structure of Post-Secondary Education in Ontario: Supplementary Report No. 1, June 1963.* Toronto: University of Toronto Press, 1963.

———. *The City College: Supplementary Report No. 2.* Toronto: University of Toronto Press, 1965.

———. *University Television: Supplementary Report No. 3.* Toronto: University of Toronto Press, 1965. The report of a subcommittee under the chairmanship of Professor D. C. Williams, University of Toronto.

GRAD, TAMARA E. "Development in Public Libraries in Ontario, Canada, 1851–1951." Unpublished M.L.S. thesis, Drexel Institute of Technology, 1952. The only account which brings the record down to recent times.

GRANT, WILLIAM L. and FREDERICK HAMILTON. *Principal Grant.* Toronto: Morang, 1904. A biography of George M. Grant, Principal of Queen's University from 1877–1902.

GUILLET, EDWIN C. *In the Cause of Education: Centennial History of the Ontario Educational Association 1861–1960.* Toronto: University of Toronto Press, 1960. A year-by-year chronicle which reflects the arguments about education within the profession and equally the relative ineffectiveness of the profession to influence the course of events.

HARDY, EDWIN A. *The Public Library: Its Place in our Educational System.* Toronto: W. Briggs, 1912.

HARRIS, ROBIN S. "The Establishment of a Provincial University in Ontario" and "The Establishment of a Provincial System of Higher Education," in D. Dadson, ed. *On Higher Education: Five Lectures.* Toronto: University of Toronto Press, 1966. The essays cover the periods 1797 to 1906, and 1906 to 1964, respectively.

HODGINS, J. GEORGE, ed. *Documentary History of Education in Upper Canada (Ontario) . . . 1791–1876.* Toronto: Warwick & Rutter, 1894–1910. 28 vols. The basic source for all matters bearing on education in the province for the period covered.

KARR, WILLIAM J. *The Training of Teachers in Ontario.* Ottawa: R. J. Taylor, 1916. A doctor of pedagogy thesis submitted to Queen's University.

MADILL, ALONZO J. *History of Agricultural Education in Ontario.* Toronto: University of Toronto Press, 1930.

MARLING, ALEXANDER. *The Canadian Educational Directory and Year Book for 1876 . . .* Toronto: Hunter Rose, 1876. A detailed description of the educational systems of the provinces of Ontario, Quebec, Nova Scotia, New Brunswick, Prince Edward Island, British Columbia, and Manitoba in the year 1876. More than half the book is devoted to Ontario. At the time of writing Marling was Chief Clerk of the Education Department of Ontario; he was Deputy Minister for a brief period in 1890.

MILLAR, JOHN. *The Educational System of the Province of Ontario.* Toronto: Education Department, 1893. A comprehensive statement of the position in 1891–2 with some account of the historical development to this point.

McCUTCHEON, JOHN M. *Public Education in Ontario.*

Toronto: T. H. Best, 1941. A competent, if pedestrian, general history of developments to 1939. There are separate chapters on elementary education, secondary education, vocational education, control, and administration, etc.

NEWCOMBE, ERVIN E. "The Development of Elementary School Teacher Education in Ontario since 1900." Unpublished doctoral dissertation, University of Toronto, 1965.

Ontario. Department of Economics. *Ontario, Economic and Social Aspects: A Survey.* Toronto: Queen's Printer, 1961.

Ontario. Department of Education. *Abstracts of the Proceedings of the Department of Education 1877–1928, together with Legislation, Reports of Literary Societies, etc.* Toronto, 1929. A year-by-year commentary which occasionally supplements the Annual Report of the Minister. A revision and extension of this abstract extending the coverage back to 1871 and on to 1958 was prepared by G. N. Bramfitt in 1960. The typescript is available from the Department of Education.

———. *Annual Report of the Minister of Education.* Toronto: Department of Education, annually 1876–1965. The Minister's *Reports* are always full of information and frequently full of interesting commentary on the failures and successes of the developing system. The same can be said of the Annual *Reports* of the Superintendent from 1845 to 1875. These are partly reproduced in Hodgins' *Documentary History.*

———. *Report of the Minister's Committee on the Training of Elementary School Teachers, 1966.* Toronto: Department of Education, 1966 (MacLeod Report).

Ontario. *Report of the Royal Commission on University Finances.* Toronto: King's Printer, 1921. 2 vols. Contains a great deal of information about Queen's

University, University of Toronto, and University of Western Ontario, particularly for the period 1900 to 1920.

PARVIN, VIOLA. *Authorization of Textbooks for the Schools of Ontario, 1846–1950.* Toronto: University of Toronto Press, 1965. A well documented study which reveals the nature and the degree of control exercised by the central authority with respect to the course of study in the elementary schools.

PORTER, JOHN. *The Vertical Mosaic: An Analysis of Social Class and Power in Canada.* Toronto: University of Toronto Press, 1965.

Report of the Grade 13 Study Committee, 1964. Toronto: Department of Education 1964. For the origin and development of Grade 13, see Chapter I.

Report of the Royal Commission on Education in Ontario. Toronto: King's Printer, 1950. A valuable document in connection with the philosophy of education in the province, and with certain aspects of its educational history, notably the separate schools and French language instruction.

SAVAGE, EDWARD G. *Secondary Education in Ontario.* London: His Majesty's Stationery Office, 1928. An assessment of secondary education in the province by an inspector of secondary schools who spent the first six months of 1926 on exchange. The picture is not flattering.

SISSONS, CHARLES B. *Bi-Lingual Schools in Canada.* London: J. M. Dent, 1917.

———. *Church and State in Canadian Education: An Historical Study.* Toronto: Ryerson, 1959. Chapter One is a detailed account of the separate school question in Ontario. Such prejudices as the author can be said to have are clearly stated.

———. *Egerton Ryerson: His Life and Letters.* Toronto:

Clarke, Irwin, 1937–49. 2 vols. The definitive study of the effective founder of the Ontario educational system.

————. *A History of Victoria University*. Toronto: University of Toronto Press, 1952.

SQUAIR, JOHN. *John Seath and the School System of Ontario*. Toronto: University of Toronto Press, 1920. A rambling account of the Ontario educational scene from 1868 to 1919 but valuable as an indication that the system did not work quite so well as its more fervent advocates—Ryerson, Ross, Seath himself—at times suggested.

ST. JOHN (Francis R.) Library Consultants, Inc. *Ontario Libraries: a Province-Wide Survey and Plan*. Toronto: Ontario Library Association, 1965.

TALMAN, JAMES J. and RUTH D. TALMAN. *Western— 1878–1953*. London: University of Western Ontario, 1953.

UNIVERSITY OF TORONTO. *University Question: the Statements of John Langton . . . and Professor Daniel Wilson . . . with Notes and Extracts from the Evidence taken before the Committee of the Legislative Assembly on the University*. Toronto: Rowsell & Ellis, 1860. The proceedings of the Select Committee, including all the evidence presented to it, were reprinted in J. G. Hodgins, ed. *Documentary History of Education in Upper Canada from . . . 1791 to . . . 1876, XV, 98–315*. Langton's statement appears at pp. 161–95, Wilson's at 207–37.

WALKER, FRANKLIN A. *Catholic Education and Politics in Upper Canada*. Toronto: Dent, 1955.

————. *Catholic Education and Politics in Ontario*. Toronto: Thomas Nelson, 1964. A thorough and scholarly study of the separate school issue from its origin in the 1840s to the 1930s when, in the author's judgement, there occurred "the last and greatest of the Roman Catholic campaigns in the political sphere."

WALLACE, W. STEWART. *A History of the University of Toronto*. Toronto: University of Toronto Press, 1927.

WEIR, GEORGE M. *Survey of Nursing Education in Canada*. Toronto: University of Toronto Press, 1932.

Notes

The Educational System of Ontario in 1965–1966

1. In 1965–6 there were 1422 Roman Catholic separate schools with an enrolment of 370,669 and two Protestant separate schools with an enrolment of 186.
2. See below 29.
3. See below 29.
4. Ontario, Department of Education. *Annual Report of the Minister of Education, 1965* (Toronto, 1965), 28–9.

The Development of the System, 1867–1966

1. Regiopolis, a Roman Catholic institution in Kingston, received a degree-granting charter in 1866 but had been incorporated since 1837. It figured prominently in discussions about the University Question throughout the 1840s. Though it undoubtedly offered some university level work in the early years, it has never granted a degree and its main role has always been that of a secondary school, a role it continues to play with distinction.
2. *Annual Report of . . . the Chief Superintendent of Education* [in Ontario] *for the year 1867* (Toronto, 1868), 23.
3. "Designed originally for the exclusive use of lumber camps the travelling libraries have extended their benefits to include lighthouse keepers on the Great Lakes, schools in isolated areas, small public libraries, women's institutes, farmers' clubs, school cars and other miscellaneous organizations with limited facilities." [J. M. McCutcheon, *Public Education in Ontario* (Toronto, 1941), 203–4.] The Provincial Library Service was still circulating some travelling libraries in 1965–6 but on a much reduced scale, the development

of regional library systems and the bookmobile having rendered them obsolescent. It is expected that the service will be withdrawn in 1967.

4. "The school car, which contains living quarters for the teacher in addition to a schoolroom compartment stops for a few days at a time at scheduled points in the isolated sections of the districts. Books and magazines are provided and radio programmes and adult evening classes are conducted. . . . Seven school cars, each in charge of a teacher specially qualified for this work, are now utilized in this important service." (*Ibid.*, 115.) In 1965–6 two railway school cars were in operation, one running from Allentown to the Manitoba border and one from Chapleau to Bolkow. Each made three stops, normally for a week at a time. Forty-four children were enrolled. The service will probably be discontinued by 1968.

5. Admission requirements are and always have been the prerogative of the individual university. Until 1896, when an Educational Council was formed to provide for common matriculation examinations, each university set its own. However, common sense was applied and there was a general recognition of transferability. The references in the paragraph are specifically to the situation at the University of Toronto and may not adhere in every particular to the situation at each of the others.

6. See below 66–70.

7. Ontario, Department of Education, *Annual Report* (Toronto, 1905), 297.

8. E. G. Savage, *Secondary Education in Ontario* (London, 1928), 67–8.

9. See above 38–9.

10. The Federation Act also made provision for federating theological colleges which were not engaged in undergraduate work. Knox and Wycliffe Colleges entered federation on this basis in 1887 and 1890 respectively. St. Michael's, which since 1881 had been affiliated to the University of Toronto, was not prepared until 1910 to offer all six of the college subjects. From 1887 on it taught some of these but not all.

11. Ontario, *Report of Royal Commission on University Finances.* Toronto, 1921. 2 vols.

12. The figures are presented solely for purposes of comparison. In 1939 Toronto also received $572,638.43 in statutory grants, for the most part related to capital expenditures. It also received grants in connection with the Royal Ontario Museum, the Connaught Laboratories, and the Ontario College of Education.

13. University of Toronto. *University Question . . .* (Toronto, 1860), 87–8.

14. See below 70–76.
15. W. L. Grant and F. Hamilton, *Principal Grant* (Toronto, 1904), 240–1.
16. *Annual Report of . . . Chief Superintendent of Education* [in Ontario] *for the year 1867*, 18. The italics are Ryerson's.
17. J. M. McCutcheon, *Public Education in Ontario* (Toronto, 1941), 217.
18. W. J. Karr, *The Training of Teachers in Ontario* (Ottawa, 1916), 9.
19. *Ibid.*, 19–34.
20. McCutcheon, *Public Education in Ontario*, 226.
21. Ontario, Department of Education, *Report of the Minister's Committee on the Training of Elementary School Teachers 1966* (Toronto, 1966), 11.
22. See above 48–9.
23. Ontario, Department of Education, *Report of the Minister's Committee 1966*, 1.
24. Hon. W. G. Davis, Minister of Education, in *Legislature of Ontario Debates*, March 29, 1966, 2009.
25. Department of Education, *Annual Report 1888*, 211.
26. John Millar, *The Educational System of Ontario* (Toronto, 1893), 111–12.
27. See above 51–6.
28. Department of Education, *Annual Report 1948*, 2.
29. Department of Education, *Annual Report 1964*, 10.
30. Committee of Presidents of Provincially Assisted Universities and Colleges of Ontario. *Post-Secondary Education in Ontario 1962–1970* (Toronto, 1963), 11–13.
31. *Ibid.*, 13.

Organization and Control, 1867–1966

1. Membership in the council was by appointment of the Lieutenant-Governor-in-Council and tended to be "permanent." Two of the original seven appointees of 1846 were still members in 1867 and a third had been a member until his death in 1866. Of the other four appointed members of the 1867 council, one had been a member since 1850, one since 1857, one since 1862—the Roman Catholic Bishop of Toronto whose predecessors in office had been members since 1846—and one since 1865. In 1874 the council was substantially increased in size by the addition, first, of three persons elected by (*a*) the public and separate school teachers, (*b*) the public school inspectors, and (*c*) the secondary school principals and teachers, and, second, of the representatives of colleges which had degree-granting powers. These latter were not, however, full

members of the council; matters relating exclusively to the public and separate schools were regarded as lying outside their jurisdiction.

2. Ontario, Department of Education, *Annual Report 1876*, 13.

3. Ontario, Department of Education, *Annual Report 1906*, iii.

4. *Ibid.*

5. Under the chief inspector were three public school, six Roman Catholic separate school, and three English-French public and separate school inspectors. There were also three high school and two continuation school inspectors.

6. In 1891 the Deputy Minister was assisted by a Chief Clerk and Accountant, the Minister's Secretary, four senior and seven junior clerks, and the Superintendent of Mechanics Institutes and Art Schools. J. G. Hodgins had been named Historiographer and Librarian, and there was an assistant librarian. In 1965 there were 3514 full-time employees of the department.

7. This legislation did not affect the separate schools, which remained under separate school boards. A Board of Education under this Act had responsibility only for the public schools, both elementary and secondary, within its jurisdiction.

8. By the terms of the Metropolitan Toronto Amendment Act (1966), the number of school boards will be reduced to six with effect January 1, 1967.

9. Preamble to Order-in-Council dated October 9, 1951.

10. Order-in-Council dated April 20, 1961.

11. Hon. M. B. Dymond, Minister of Health, in *Legislature of Ontario Debates*, April 19, 1966, 2459.

Index

CANADIAN UNIVERSITY PAPERBOOKS

Other titles in the series

Lightning Source UK Ltd.
Milton Keynes UK
UKHW020021210722
406167UK00009B/783